...to The Ichthus File

We hope you enjoy it. Before you start, you'll need:

A BIBLE Get a readable version, like the NIV (New International Version)

A PEN It helps to write answers down, as well as things you want to remember or to pray for each day. Write in the File itself or in your own notebook.

A CLOCK Aim for 10-15 mins on each study at the start or end of your day. Don't get hung up if you miss a day- just get going again.

A BRAIN You'll have to think about the Bible passage and about how you might need to change. Think as you ask God to help you at the start of each study and when you pray at the end.

THE ICHTHUS FILE It's hip to be square! Yes, it is!

Welcome, one and all. Here's a handy Q & A page to help you gain the most from the big square:

1. WHY'S IT CALLED THE ICHTHUS FILE?

Well, long story, but the short answer is this: it's a great name, let's face it. 'Ichthus' is ancient Greek for fish. And it's an acronym (not acrobat) for 'Jesus Christ, God's Son, Saviour'. So The Ichthus File points you, as the Bible does, to Jesus.

2. WHAT DO I NEED BEFORE I START?

Er, you need the colossal initiative to read page 1 first...

3. WHAT ARE THE SQUARE EYES FOR?

This symbol means: please read from the Bible.

This means: slow down and think this stuff over.

This means: take this truth to your life. Apply it.

This means: pray. That's you talking to God.

4. WHAT CAN I EXPECT TO HAPPEN AS I READ THE BIBLE?

Thunderbolts? Hair standing up on the back of your neck? Er, maybe, but unlikely. Expect to meet with God. The Bible is God speaking. Now that's some prospect. So get ready to be encouraged, challenged, unsettled, provoked, surprised - and urged to keep living for Jesus.

5. WHAT ON EARTH ARE OPTIONAL EXTRAS?

Unsurprisingly, they're bits designed for those who want to take each study to a greater depth. They're at the back of the issue: each study tells you which page to go to. Oh, you'll find our studies in Psalms don't have Opt Extras. Now you know.

6. ANY LAST PIECES OF ADVICE?

Sure. As you weave your way through Romans and 1 Kings, why not dip into a psalm in between? It's entirely up to you: you choose the pace you'd like to go at.

Enjoy!

NEWS FOR THE WORLD

Romans 1-8 - introduction

Here's a letter to make you go: **Aaargh! Oh! Mmm! Eh? Nzzz.** OK, we'll explain. You make the noises, we'll do the talking...

AAARGH!

You'll say this in a few days' time when you wail: 'Why haven't I got my face into Romans before now? If only I'd known...'

OH!

If you do, you'll merely be joining bus-loads of people spread over almost 20 centuries who are convinced that Romans is the most significant book they've *ever* read.

MMM!

Some have come to trust in Jesus for the first time 'cos of it. Some are stunned at the way it sharpens truths about God and people. Some find their faith unexpectedly shaken to life as never before. What will Romans be for you?

EH?

Romans presents the gospel - God's good news for the world - in all its glory. And then slaps down the implications of that.

You think that doesn't sound like much? You think God's anger is trivial? Or God's love is cheap? Or God's grace is pretty irrelevant? You think the cross is a little sideshow? You think you're sorted as a Christian?

Get your adrenalin dose thru' Romans' stress on the gospel.

NZZZ...

Romans is powerful 'cos it's in-depth. So it won't let you doze. (Er, OK, Nzzz = 'no sleep'. Of course!)

We've just spent a whole intro page not telling you much about Romans. All we've been is uncontrollably excited about it.

That's entirely deliberate. And we hope it might be your reaction once you've stashed God's good news from chs. 1-8 into your Christian life.

* Wait for Romans 9-16 in a future issue of *The Ichthus File*.

OUTWARD BOUND
Romans - background

The letter of Romans: the who, who, when, why, how, wow.

Who?

Paul the apostle wrote it. He was the one specially by Jesus (see 1 v1, 11 v13, 15 v15-16) to take the good news of the cross to Gentiles (ie, anyone who's not a Jew.)

Who 2?

Paul's writing (1 v7) to Christians in Rome (centre of the world then). ie, he's writing to ordinary people, like you and me. Paul didn't start the church there, but he was about to visit it.

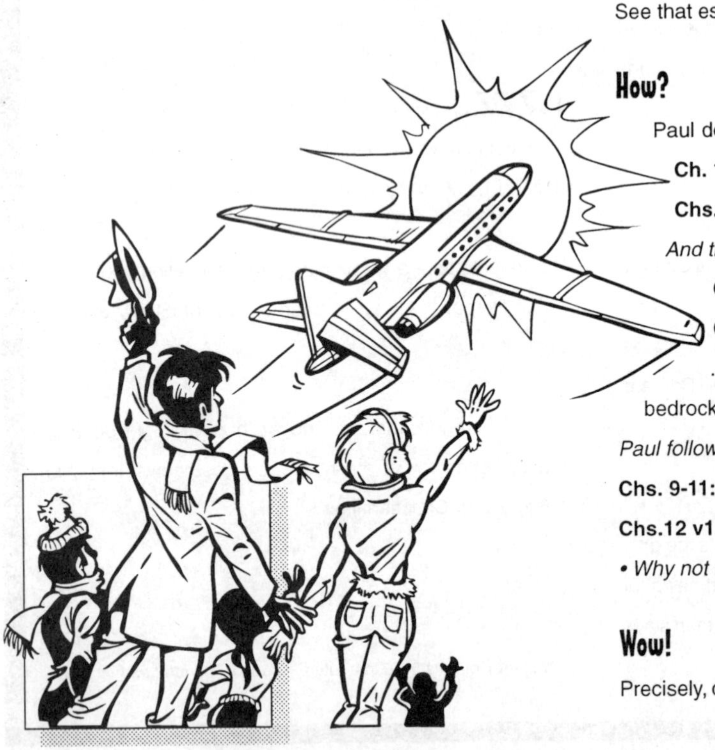

It was a church made up essentially of Gentile Christians. See that, eg, in 1 v13 and 11 v13.

When?

It's the mid-to-late 50s AD. Paul was in Corinth at the time (see Acts 20 v1-3) - just before he'd return to Jerusalem.

Why?

Paul wants this Gentile church to grab hold of its responsibility towards other members of God's people. In this case, to step outward to Jews - across a whopping cultural divide. See that especially in chs. 9-11: wait for the next issue!

How?

Paul does this as follows. He starts and ends like this:

Ch. 1 v1-17: intro

Chs. 15 v14-16v27: Paul's plans and greetings

And the middle bit's like this:

Chs. 1 v18 - 3 v20: God's anger

Chs. 3 v21 - 8 v39: God's grace

... ie, that's the gospel! This is the foundation. The bedrock.

Paul follows that with its implications for:

Chs. 9-11: Jews - God's Old T people

Chs.12 v1 - 15 v13: Christians - all God's people

• *Why not take a bite from each section to get the flavour?*

Wow!

Precisely, old bean. Come for a run down the Rome straight...

OPEN TO OFFER
Romans 1 v1-7

When you write letters, it's probably in this pattern:

Dear Wendy, blurby, blurby, blurby, blurby, blurby, love John.

Except if your name's not John, that is.

At the time the apostle Paul was writing, it was this pattern:

John to Wendy: blurby, blurby etc.

Now peek at Romans 1 v1 and v7. See the pattern there?

Of course. But what's all that stuff between v1 and v7, then? Well, it's Paul introducing himself. The pattern's like this:

John (lawyer, dad, Christian) to Wendy: blurby, blurby, etc.

Paul didn't start the church in Rome - he hadn't even visited it - so he needed to let them know who he was. Let's find out...

Read Romans 1 v1-7.

Me, him, you

• *In what two ways does he briefly introduce himself (v1)?*

Then Paul gets carrried away (v1b-2) by the gospel: it's tub-thumpingly great stuff, he says (OK, 'gospel' = good news).

• *Who's it from, says Paul (v1b)? And who's it about (v3a)?*

• *Why can we trust it (v2)?*

Pick out the facts we're told about Jesus in v3.

• *But is that the whole story about him (v4)?*

• *How can we be sure of all this (v4)?*

• *What's Jesus status now (v4b)? What does that mean?*

v5: Paul describes his job.

• *What is it, then? And who employed him?*

• *Who does he say this good news is for (v5)?*

• *What's the only right, ongoing response to Jesus (v5)?*

Notice how Paul describes the Roman Christians (v6, 7)?

• *What does he pray for them (v7b)?*

Short but huge intro. That's Paul for you. And that's Romans. Paul can't help but shout about the gospel. More next!

• *Hang on, has the gospel gripped you?*

• *Do you believe it's good news for everybody?*

Tell God your answer. And pray Romans would change you.

For further study see the **OPTIONAL EXTRA** on page 55

ROAM SWEET ROME

Romans 1 v8-17

Intro over - on with the blurby bit. It's more personal stuff from Paul: 'I this...', 'I that...' and 'I aye...' (er, Scottish translation).

• *Given v1-6, what do you expect Paul to talk about most?*

Read Romans 1 v8-13.

Paul's plan

Rome was capital of the world, then: hub of everything.

• *So why's Paul right to be thankful to God (v8)?*

Grief, he even prayed for Christians he'd never met (v10a). Bag two reasons why Paul wanted to get to Rome (v11,13).

• *What did he hope to receive from the Christians there (v12)?*

Read v14-17.

God's gift

Note down the three things Paul says about himself ('I...'):

v14a:

v15a:

v16a:

Now express them a different way, in your own words.

• *Could you say 'I...' as Paul does here?*

• *Why, like Paul, should we tell others about Jesus (v14)?*

It's an obligation. A duty. We owe it to people, says Paul. God's entrusted us, too, with his gospel: so pass it on, folks.

Think how we're tempted to be ashamed of the gospel.

• *Why mustn't we be (v16)?*

• *Who would you say needs the gospel? Who does Paul?*

Read v17 again: what does the gospel bring (v17)?

• *How is this obtained (v17b)?*

Thru' the gospel, God puts us in the clear with him. Says we're back on terms, right with him. Pure, in his opinion.

Some gift!

Now answer: how must I change my attitude to the gospel?

• *Could I say v16-17 with the conviction Paul does?*

For further study see the **OPTIONAL EXTRA** on page 55

OVER AND OUT

Romans 1 v18-32 (part 1)

Paul's just said (1 v16) that salvation's open to anyone. ie, thru' the gospel, *anyone* can know God's rescue.

Great... but why does anyone *need* it? What would you say?

• *Why do people need Jesus?*

Paul proves his case in the rest of chs. 1, 2 & 3. With relentless logic. We've spread this study over two pages. Go steady.

Read Romans 1 v18-20.

Wicked isn't cool

See why people need God's rescue, according to v18a?

• *Why is God angry at human beings (v18b-19)?*

• *Why should we know better than to walk out on God (v20)?*

What's one way we know God exists? The world around us.

• *How should this make us respond to God (clue in v20a)?*

It means no-one can say: 'Sorry, God, I'd no idea you were there.' But people live as if that was true. Right?

God's not just angry (and rightly so) about that, he's judging us for it (v18a). Now. In thunderbolts? No. Like this...

Read v21-24.

Note the three steps (here and in the next sections):

1. Ongoing human action: v21b, 22b, 23

2. Reason why this is hideously wrong: v21a

3. God's ongoing response: v24

Read v25-27.

1. v25a:

2. v25b:

3. v26-27:

Read v28-32.

1. v28a, 32b:

2. v32a:

3. v28b-31:

Fearsome stuff, this. Re-read your three answers to point 3: 'God gave them over... gave them over... gave them over.'

• *To what?*

• *What do all your answers to pt 3 have in common?*

(Join us on the next page... no Opt Ex till then. Cheers.)

TRAMPLING TRUTH

Romans 1 v18-32 (part 2)

On for more? Good.

• *What is it that God has 'given us over to' for rejecting him?*

GOD'S

Well, what v24, 26 and 28 have in common is this: God's judging us *already* - and his way of doing that is to abandon us to our own self-centredness. It means, in effect, God gives us what we want.

• *Why is that seriously bad news?*

See the repeated word 'exchanged' (v23, 25, 26)?

• *Just how beltingly stupid is what we've chosen?*

Remember the horrific result of all this (24-25, 26-27, 28-31)?

ANGER

Paul spells it out. God's judgment leads to...

v24: the abuse of sex;

v26: lesbian/homosexual relationships;

v28-31: social breakdown.

Get the picture? ie, inside and out, we're twisted.

IS

v32: Paul says it's written into every conscience that God will judge evil. Catch his 1, 2, 3 summary again:

1. People choose to bury the fact God exists...

2. ... although they know God exists as their judge.

3. So God's right to maintain his anger against them.

Get his point? None of us has lived up to what we know of God. But we've deliberately shunted him out of our lives. We can't plead ignorance. Or make other excuses, either.

ON SHOW

God's not an idle spectator on his world. Or indifferent to evil. He's expressing his anger for all to see. One day, he'll carry out a final judgment. And v18-32 have told us the charge.

In God's court, we're guilty. And without an excuse to offer. He's angry with us.And demonstrating it.

• *Beginning to see why we need Jesus?*

Talk to God about your reaction to this passage.

For further study see the **OPTIONAL EXTRA** on page 56

INESCAPABLE, INEXCUSABLE

Romans 2 v1-16

Ever hear someone giving directions say: 'You can't miss it'? How often, with tennis on TV say, do you shout 'Oi, that ball was out!' before the replay showed the line judge was right? How glad are you when a teacher doesn't show favouritism?

Paul's subject last time was God's anger. Next it's the day of God's final judgment. He's saying: 'You won't miss it.' And: 'There'll be no mistakes.' And: 'No favourites, either.'

Read Romans 2 v1-4.

NO ESCAPE

• *Who's Paul talking to now (v1a)?*

It's like he's saying: 'OK, anyone who's got the ability to criticise everyone else except themselves, listen in.'

• *See yourself here, perhaps?*

• *What's he saying to such people (v1b, 3)?*

See the mistake those people make (v4): thinking God's soft - so they can carry on just as they are.

Read v5-11.

NO INJUSTICE

• *What's the danger for such people (v5)?*

• *What will be God's judgment be like (v6)?*

Use v7-11 to describe the 2 groups of people; the 2 results. Get the hint? Christians must show their faith in Jesus by persevering in doing stuff that pleases him.

Read v12-16.

NO FAVOURITES

Seems tricky to follow. Stick with it.

The Jews were given the Law (Ten Commandments etc).

• *But what's true of everybody (v14-15)?*

Right! We're made by God, so each of us has an in-built idea of his requirements. It's called conscience. And Paul's saying we'll all be judged by God according to what we know (v12). And we're all guilty of not living up to what we know of God.

• *How devastatingly thorough will God's judgment be (v16)?*

• *What has today's slice of Romans brought home to you?*

For further study see the **OPTIONAL EXTRA** on page 56

SHAKEY JAKEY

Romans 2 v17 - 3 v8

> **Dear Paul,**
> OK, pal, you've shown (1 v18-32) how the godless Gentile world (every non-Jew) is inexcusably guilty in front of God. And those who think they're OK - when they're not (2 v1-16).
>
> That's all fair enough. But we're Jews, Paul. Members of the people God chose. He gave *us* his law, gave *us* the sign of circumcision to show we were his. We're set apart, Paul.
>
> **Yours frankly, Jake the Jew**

Shrewd cookie that he is, Paul writes a swift reply...

Read Romans 2 v17-24.

Jake the fake

- *What's Paul criticism of these over-confident Jews (v21)?*
- *What's the terrible result of their actions (v24)?*

Memo to Jake: teaching others, are you? Well, start living it. You're not living up to the knowledge of God he's given you.

Read v25-29.

Jake the break

Circ. was the sign of being a member of God's people.

- *But would it guarantee protection from God's anger (v25)?*

Paul's saying: physical circ. was never enough *on its own.*

- *What does God look for (v25a, 29)?*

Memo, part two: So, Jake, thinking that circ. is your ticket to be 'in' with God is badly wrong. God's not interested first in what a person's like outwardly. Sort your heart out. Or you'll be under God's condemnation - just like everyone else.

Dangers for us to pick up here:

- *Are you beginning to congratulate yourself?*

- *Do you think you deserve preferential treatment from God?*

- *Are you practising what you preach?*

We're self-deceived if we think 'God's judgment could never happen to me.' Got that?

We'll scoop up ch. 3 v1-8 in the Opt Extra. Oh yes we will.

For further study see the **OPTIONAL EXTRA** on page 57

NO WIN NO-ONE

Romans 3 v9-20

In ch. 1, Paul said Gentiles deserve God's judgment - for not living up to their (in-built) knowledge of God.

In chs. 2 & 3, he's just said it's the same for Jews: they've failed to live up to the Old T law God gave them..

Jews, Gentiles: does that miss anyone out? Sum it up, Paul...

Read Romans 3 v9-20.

v9: everybody

'Are we any better?' ie, 'we apostles' (Paul & co), that is.

• What's Paul's conclusion here?

• What's it mean to be 'under sin' (v9b)?

Er, burdened by it, crushed, trapped, weighed down. Yeah?

Next Paul backs up his point. And again. And again. And...

v10-18: that's everybody

'Righteous' = here living fully as God wants.

• Why on earth does Paul give seven Old T quotes?

Scoop out what the following verses have in common:

v11b, 18 v13-15, 18b v10-12

v19-20: yes, everybody

v19a: 'law' here = the whole Old T. It can't save people - 'cos no-one can keep its standards. It only highlights our wrong.

• Can anyone speak up before God and claim a special case?

• Where does that leave absolutely everybody (v19b)?

EVERYBODY

Let's sum up, too:

v11b-18: our crime is playing God: me rules, OK?

v13-15, 18b: every aspect of our lives is tainted: speech, actions, mind, will, emotions, conscience, you name it.

v10-12: everyone's included. And no exceptions.

Therefore... you and I desperately need to hear the gospel.

Paul's said he'd got God's good news for us. That's next.

• See where we'd be without it (v19b)?

Don't skip on so fast you fail to accept God's verdict on us. It's on you, too (v10).

• Why do we always want to make excuses? Why can't we?

Take your response to God.

For further study see the OPTIONAL EXTRA on page 57

Bite the But

Romans 3 v21-31

Clinical conclusion: a whole worldful of people condemned by God. And with no flicker of hope. End of story?

Read Romans 3 v21-26.

But now...

Here's a double page on it all. Start with this, slowly...

v21: But (*whoa, guys, it's not the end of the story*)
now (ie, in what Jesus has done)
a righteousness from God (God declaring us right with him)
apart from law (ie, it's not by clocking up good works)
has been made known (*yahoo!*)
to which the Law and the Prophets testify (ie, clearly point).

v22: This righteousness comes from God (*superb!*)
thru' faith in Jesus Christ (us relying on him)
to all who believe (yes, it's open to all)
There is no difference (between Jew or Gentile or anybody)

v23: for all have sinned (yes, they - we - have)
and fall short of the glory of God (yes, they - we - still do)

v24: and are justified (declared innocent by God)
freely (*too right it is*)
by his grace (God's no-holds-barred generosity)
thru' the redemption (payment that brought our freedom)
that came by Jesus Christ (he paid what it took).

v25: God presented him as a sacrifice of atonement (God sent his Son to die to take away God's anger against us)
thru' faith (yep, trust)
in his blood (his death on the cross).
He did this to demonstrate his justice (and so his integrity)
because in his forbearance (patience)
he had left the sins committed beforehand unpunished (ie, all the sins of the world before the time of Jesus' cross)

v26: he did it to demonstrate his justice (*repeat for effect*)
at the present time (time of Jesus' death)
so as to be just (to show his hatred and judgment of evil)
and the one who justifies (to show his love for his people)
the man who has faith in Jesus (*incredible result, eh?*).

• What do you find unstoppably brilliant about these verses?

Cross Channel

Romans 3 v21-31 (part two)

Somebody once said (cor, we've done our research well) that Romans 3 v21-26 was the most important paragraph *ever* written. Would you agree? Maybe... after a closer peek at it.

Re-read v21-26.

Revealed

• *What's the good news in these verses? C'mon, explain it...*

The cross of Jesus reveals a righteousness from God: his gift of declaring us back in his favour: his 'justifying' us.

• *So what does the cross tell us about God?*

Ch. 3 v9 told us we're trapped by our sin. Caught by it.

• *But what has Jesus done (v24)?*

Chs 1-3 told us we each deserve God's anger. His wrath. So... how can God now just declare us 'all clear' with him?

• *What has happened to God's anger (v25)?*

God didn't change his mind. Or get forgetful. Or just pretend we're not that bad after all. No, Jesus took God's anger. God channeled it onto his Son.

Check v26, and think how the cross shows:

a) God's justice (that he must punish sin)

b) God's love (that he wants to put us right with him)

It's Jesus, God's perfect Son, who takes God's punishment and dies *instead of us.* That's nothing short of awesome.

Read v27-31.

Defended

Paul lists 3 objections (v27a, 29a, 31) that Jews might make to this great gospel - and answers them (v28, 29b-30, 31b).

• *Why does faith in Jesus rule out pride (v27b-28)?*

• *Who's the gospel for (v30)?*

• *So can we trust in Jesus and go on living as we like (v31)?*

'Cos of what God has done... there's no room for puffing yourself up, excluding others, or careless living.

• *Instead, what impact should this great gospel have on us?*

Make a point of thanking God for the thunderingly good news this paragraph tells us about.

For further study see the **OPTIONAL EXTRA** on page 58

ABRAHAM LINK ON

Romans 4 v1-15

Phew. Big truth, that. Paul makes it easier now. He illustrates this 'justification by faith' business with a guy you might know. Brain feeling sleepy? Stick it into these three big questions...

Read Romans 4 v1-8.

WORKS JERKS

It's Abe, OK? Colossal figure in the story of God's people.

1. Was Abe justified by doing the right stuff (v2-3)?

Yes **No** **Uh, eh?**

See the shocking truth in v5? God justifies his *enemy* (the 'wicked') when that person trusts God for his rescue.

• *See what the result is (v7-8)?*

The great King David knew v8 to be true for himself. Do you? That's what trusting God, being justified, brings. Topsville.

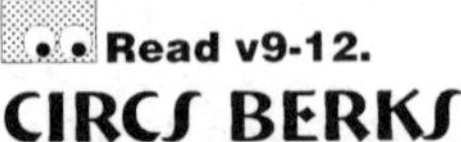

Read v9-12.

CIRCS BERKS

2. Was Abe justified 'cos of his circumcision (v10b-11)?

Yes **No** **Sorry, I was dozing**

• *Why is all this encouraging for us (v11b)?*

• *Whose father is Abe, then (v11-12)?*

Read v13-15.

HMMM...

Blown it. Can you think of a third rhyming heading? We can't.

3. Was Abe justified by obeying God's law?

Yes **No** **zzzzzzzz**

v13: ie, it was a promise from God, not a law with conditions God wasn't saying to Abe 'Obey this law and I'll bless you.' But: 'I will bless you. Believe my promise.'

• *See the difference?*

• *What's it tell us about God and the right response to him?*

4. Was Abe justified by faith, then?

Yes **Yes** **Wait for next time!**

Thank God for reminders that we can't save ourselves. Right?

For further study see the **OPTIONAL EXTRA** on page 58

CREDIT, NOTE

Romans 4 v16-25

PROMISES, PROMISES...

If some bloke you met in the street made this promise to you:

'I'm going to give you ten million dollars next Christmas.'

a) Would you believe him? Why/why not?

b) If your best friend said it, would you believe him/her? Why/why not?

Now, we suspect... you wouldn't trust the bloke (a). You don't know if he's trustworthy or able (ie, got enough cash) to keep his promise.

And you would like to trust your friend (b). You know (we hope...) he/she's pretty trustworthy. But you doubt they've got the dosh. Or that they'd give it to you...

But if he/she promised: 'I'll give you a top Christmas present' - you'd trust him/her. You know your friend's reliable. And able to keep it. Right?

What about God's promises? Is he reliable? Is he able to keep them? Back to the illustration on Abraham...

Read v16-17.

FACE GRACE

v16: ie, God's grace makes promises. We're to believe 'em. See who they're for (v16b) and how reliable God is: he made a promise to Abe (v17a) and kept it - we're proof of that (v16b).

- *See how powerful God is, too (v17b)?*

Read v18-25.

FAITH LIFT

- *What characterised Abe's faith (v18a, 19a, 20a, 21a)?*

Abe looked at a doubly impossible situation (v19) in the light of the promises God gave him (v17a, 18b).

- *What was the result for Abe (v22)?*
- *What does Abe's example illustrate for us now (v23-24)?*

See God's promise (v25)? God will justify us (instead of rightly condemn us forever): Jesus' resurrection declares that. So... believe the promise. Trust God! He's reliable. And he's able to keep his promise: the resurrection shows that.

v25's worth storing away in your head (go on, do). And thank God for his promise to put us right with him. It's *true*.

- *What will you now say to God?*

For further study see the **OPTIONAL EXTRA** on page 58

CAUGHT DISTRAUGHT

Psalm 61

Do real men cry?

☐ Yes ☐ No

Do real men admit difficulties?

☐ Yes ☐ No

Do real men pray?

☐ Yes ☐ No

Now, any point to those questions? Er, maybe.

King David was God's all-conquering (almost) King. A hero? A real man? But what was this big enemy-basher *really* like?

This psalm gives us a glimpse of David - sort-of inside out:

Read Psalm 61.

WATCH HIM PRAY

What impression do you get of David here? Note down...

His current situation (clues in v1-2, 4):

His memories (v3, 5):

His requests (v1, 2b, 6-7):

His hopes (v4):

His promises (v8):

WHAT'S HE SAY?

v1-2: feel David's distance from God - and need of him? 'Lead me to the rock...' ie, 'I can't get there myself, God.'

v3: the rock of v2 is God. David sees himself as a refugee.

• *What truths about God is he sure of (v3b-4)?*

v5: might refer to David's crowning as king, when he made vows and was given responsibility to lead God's people. ie, he's remembering what God's done in the past.

• *Confident of that, what did he ask for the future (v6-7)?*

• *And how would he show his gratitude to God (v8)?*

Think what David, in despair, remembered about God: what he's like, and what he's done in the past.

Why not pray that God will help you turn *to* him, not *away* from him, when things get hard?

* More on v5 and v8: hmm, past vows aren't enough. There was to be an ongoing obedience to God. Agree?

WORDS FOR NERDS

Psalm 62

'God's just a crutch for people who can't handle life,' it's said. ie, only inadequate nerds go about pretending there's a God - 'cos they're not big enough to face life by themselves.

• Do you agree or disagree? Why?

Psalm 62 would answer that question. Probably like this:

• You'd be a nerd to ignore the fact there is a God.

• You'd be a nerd to ignore what he's like.

• You'd be a nerd to ignore what he's said.

• You'd be a nerd to think life's always easy to cope with.

ie, you'd be a nerd to believe that view expressed above.

Don't be a nerd and not read the psalm then...

Read Psalm 62.

ROYAL REFUGEE

v1-2, 6-8: trust. Explain, please, what king David was sure of (v1-2, 6-7).

• What had he discovered God to be like?

• What did this make him do (v8)?

David said (v1): 'my salvation (rescue) comes *from* God'... and also 'God *is* my salvation' (v2).

• What's he saying then about God?

v3-5: trouble. Use v3-4 to see why David needed to remind himself (in v5) to keep trusting God. (Imagine who he's talking to in v3-4.)

v9-12: truth. See how those who don't trust God have no stability (v9-10)?

David recognised three things (yes, one plus two, v11): God is powerful, loves his people and is a God of judgment. So it's not only good to trust God. It's vital we do. David was no nerd. He relied on God. What about you?

• Do you do what he says in v8?

Sounds strange to talk about your soul like David did (v1).

• But will you thank God for his hold on us, as David did?

• Is God your refuge - in reality or just in theory?

THE GOODY BAG

Romans 5 v1-11

Paul's just been saying we're 'justified by faith': we're declared right with God as we trust in the cross of Jesus. Not to be condemned by God as we deserve. All clear!

Now he tells us more goodies that come with being justified.

Read Romans 5 v1-8.

SWEET STUFF

- *What do those who trust Jesus now have (v1b)?*
- *What other privilege is ours (v2)?*

Peace with God: a restored relationship. And we're 'in grace': on the receiving end of God's give, give, give generosity.

- *What should this make us do (v2b)? Why?*
- *What else can we get excited about (v3)? Incredibly, why?*

Joy: a deep-seated celebration. And hope: the anticipation of sharing God's glory. But how can we be sure of this?

Well, how do we know God loves us (v8, 5b)?

- *What did Christ do for us, and when (v8)?*
- *And what has God done for each of us (v5b)?*

Simple! We know God loves us 'cos his own Son Jesus died for us - while we were God's enemies. And God's given his Spirit to all who trust him. Rock and roll!

But there are more goodies...

Read v9-11.

TASTY TREATS

v9 talks of the final day when God will judge his world.

- *What's true for those who trust in Jesus' cross (v9)?*
- *Why can we be sure of this (v10)?*

See... if God's done the difficult thing (v10a), of course we can be sure he'll complete the job and hold onto us when his judgment comes (v10b).

And there's even more to get excited about (v11). Yeah?

Think what you'll be thanking God for from v1-11.

And do it.

For further study see the OPTIONAL EXTRA on page 59

PEOPLEWATCH
Romans 5 v12-21

Seen those nature progs where boffins who can't say their r's wummage about in the undergwowth looking at wemarkable communities of animals? OK. Maybe not. No big deal. Join Paul as he turns the camera on two communities: Adam's people and Christ's people.

Read Romans 5 v12-14.

INTRODUCTIONS, PLEASE

v12: it's a rather cool unfinished sentence which Paul

• *But what's his point?*

Adam (the 'one man') disobeyed God. God's punishment was death: Adam died. All that's true for every human since. So...

First community: Adam's people

Who's included: everyone **Main features:** sin, death

• *But how does Adam point us forward (v14b)?*

Read v15-17.

SPOT THE DIFFERENCE

OK. Fill in the gaps:

Second community: Christ's people

Who's included (v17a): **Main features** (v16b, 17b):

Spot the peppy phrase 'how much more...' (v15, 17)?

• *How is what Jesus did better (v15), more wide-reaching (v16) and more effective (v17) than what Adam did?*

And all this is on offer for those who become members of Christ's people. That's those who receive God's great gift (v17) - being declared right with God as they trust Jesus.

Read v18-21.

NOTE THE SIMILARITY

Both Jesus and Adam had a huge effect on lots of people by a single act. What did each of them do to have this effect?

• *And what were the results?*

Christians are Adam's people, sure. But we're also Christ's. We've been given life forever - instead of death! Feel free to break into a celebratory shimmy around the room at this point. Then stop to thank the man who made it possible.

For further study see the **OPTIONAL EXTRA** on page 59

TWIN PEAKS

Romans 6 v1-14

A pair of twins look the same, sound the same, but aren't the same age. They were born years apart. The first one died at exactly the time the other was born. How can this be?
Simple. They're both you! And both me! Maybe this will help:

Read Romans 6 v1-4.

Dying down

Paul's answering people who say: 'OK, so you mean we can sin all we like and God will still show grace to forgive us?'

• *How does Paul say that's wrong wrong wrong (v2)?*

See how we're counted as having 'died to sin' (v3b, 4a)?

• *What should this lead to then (v4b)?*

(Baptism? Check the Opt Ex.)

Paul's saying this: those who trust Jesus have *shared in* Jesus's own death and *shared in* his resurrection.

Just stop and swallow that for a minute.

Read v5-10.

Dead and alive

Now the twins come in. Twin one is our 'old self' (v6). It dies when we trust Jesus (and so share in his death). Twin two is born (as we share in Jesus' resurrection, ie a new life - v5, 8). ie, our old self's gone. We're now living to please God.

• *What's happened to twin one (v6)?*

• *Who does twin two live for (v10)?*

Read v11-14.

Living it out

• *Negatively, what does Paul here tell the Christian not to do?*

• *Positively, what is the Christian told to do?*

It's going to be hard: so don't miss the great promise (v14). If you're a Christian, you're twin two. So live like it: get pleasing God and root out the wrong in your life.

Don't think about going back to being twin one. How could you when you've *shared in* Jesus' death and resurrection?

• *How will you take up the challenge of v12 then?*

For further study see the **OPTIONAL EXTRA** on page 59

SLAVING - A WAY

Romans 6 v15-23

Pat yourself on the back. Go on. Romans is in-depth stuff. And you're doing well. Hope you're enjoying it, too. Now...

Welcome to Honest John's New and Used Slave Mart.

'But I don't want any slaves!'

That's OK, we don't sell them. You're here as a slave. You just have to choose a master!

Read Romans 6 v15-18.

Freedom is slavery

Last time, Paul smashed the objection ('does grace encourage sin?') with the answer ('No! We're united with Christ.'). Here, it's practically the same question. But a different reply. It's all about slavery.

- *What is the choice of masters on offer (v16)?*
- *What change in our ownership has taken place (v17)?*

Everyone's a slave. When we trust in Jesus, we're set free from one master (sin), to become slaves to another: God.

- *So can we now just live as we please? Why not?*

Read v19-23.

Slavery is freedom

v19: both sets of slaves become more like their masters.

- *How should you be making progress then?*

Note the benefit in being a slave to sin:

Now (v20, 21):

Ultimately (v21b, 23):

And the benefit in being a slave to God:

Now (v22):

Ultimately (v22b, 23b):

- *What does each slave receive from his master (v23)?*

Spot the difference: one master pays wages (what's deserved), the other presents a gift (what's not deserved).

So... slavery to God is more like freedom. Right?

Since, as Christians, we've given ourselves over to serve Christ, get on with it. Don't go back to sin, your old boss.

Talk to God about where you're not measuring up.

For further study see the **OPTIONAL EXTRA** on page 60

Two weddings and a Funeral

Romans 7 v1-6

They make adults cry. They keep dressmakers in business. They make you miss Saturday telly. Weddings: love 'em!

Paul never married himself (or anyone else, boom boom) but he'd got a lot to say about weddings anyway...

Read Romans 7 v1-3.

Wife line

v1: he's writing to Christians who know the law (ie, the Old T law given by God to his people via Moses).

- *What's Paul's main point (v1b)?*

- *How does his story (v2-3) illustrate that?*

See how long God's law says two people are married for (v2).

- *When can a woman marry for a second time without committing adultery (v3)?*

Great, but what's that got to do with anything, Paul?

Read v4-6.

Fruit punch

- *What truth about the Christian life was Paul teaching (v4)?*

Ah! Our situation as Christians is similar to the widow who remarries. 'Cos we 'died' (when we shared in Jesus' death), we're released from our old 'marriage' (that tied us to sin and death, v5) and we've a new partner.

- *Whom do we now belong to (v4)? What should result (v4b)?*

ie, we're to be fruitful, productive for God.

- *What we were like before we became Christians (v5)?*

- *Who helps us to be useful for God now?*

v6: now that the law has no hold on us, we're free to serve God *far* more effectively. With the Holy Spirit's help we're better able to live our lives in the way the law demanded. Cool!

Talk to God about how fruitful you are for him, and how fruitful you would like to be.

For further study see the **OPTIONAL EXTRA** on page 60

Law on Trial

Romans 7 v7-25

Paul now picks up another crit that might have been lobbed at him: 'So, Paul, are you blaming everything on the law? You say Christians are free from it (7 v4) - but it's God's law, mate. Are you now saying we should chuck it?'

Read Romans 7 v7-13.

Law defended

Spot the verses here show the law...

reveals sin; provokes sin; condemns sin.

Geddit? So the law's OK in itself (v12). It's us and our sinful natures that get tripped up by it and so disobey God and come under his judgment.

Read v14-25.

Law exposed

It's likely (if you want to argue, then *outside*) Paul's talking here about himself just *before* he came to trust in Christ:

- He knew God's law and liked it (v18b, 22).
- But he was still a slave to sin (v14-15, 19-20, 23).

So Paul's saying: 'OK, so the law may be holy, but it couldn't help me be holy one little bit.'

- *What did he long for (v24) Why?*
- *What did he recognise he needed (v25)?*

That's where Romans 8 kicks in. Only Jesus, and his Spirit living in us, can help us live as God wants. Wait 'n' see!
You may not have realised it, but you have just read one of the snortiest, tricky chapters in the Bible. Well done.

Paul's main argument is clear, tho':
The real problem for people isn't the law. It's sin in us.
The law can't save us 'cos we can't keep it.
We can't keep it 'cos of indwelling sin.

Which is why ch. 8's talk of God's Spirit living in us comes as such good news. Thank God that Jesus' cross went to the heart of the problem.

For further study see the **OPTIONAL EXTRA** on page 60

SPIRIT SPECIAL

Romans 8 v1-17

Ch. 8's a stonker. A stormer. It's, er, we're lost for words. The law couldn't save us, 'cos of our sin, ch. 7 said. Cue ch. 8...

Read Romans 8 v1-4.

FREED

• *What must every Christian remember (v1)? Why (v2)?*

The gospel ('the law of the Spirit of life') has done what the Old T law could never do (v3a): bring us rescue! And all thru' Jesus taking God's punishment instead of us (v3b).

• *So what marks out the Christian (v4b)?*

Read v5-11.

CONTROLLED

Be a luv. Please jot down from v5-8:

The 2 categories of people:

The 2 perspectives:

The 2 ways of life:

The 2 destinies:

• *What's big-time encouraging for the Christian here (v9)?*

• *What does God's Spirit in us guarantee (v9b, 10, 11b)?*

Read v12-17.

ENCOURAGED

Since God's Spirit in us has given us life, we can't possibly go on living as we please. What's our duty now (v12, 13b)?

• *Are we left to do this alone (v13)?*

• *What are the sins you need to cut out of your life, with the Spirit's help?*

See, fantastically, what else God's Spirit does in us:

v15a:

v16:

• *And what's the consequence of all this (v17)?*

• *What will this mean for the life now and for the future?*

Thank God for the work of his Spirit in us, his children. Tell him the things you need the Spirit's help to change.

For further study see the **OPTIONAL EXTRA** on page 61

GROAN ZONE

Romans 8 v18-27

Last time, Paul talked about Christians sharing God's glory.

I'll have some of that please.

And about sharing Christ's sufferings, too.

Oh. Hang on. Maybe I, er, um.

But that's the pattern for us, too. Sufferings before glory...

Read Romans 8 v18.

FUTURE FOCUS

Expecting life to be a breeze? Tough luck, matey. Paul clearly expects Christians to suffer with the kind of things that affect everyone: illnesses, pain, injustice and school dinners.

• *But how should v18 transform our attitude to them?*

One day God's glory won't be revealed to us, but *in* us. God will finish making us like him. We'll be his glory!

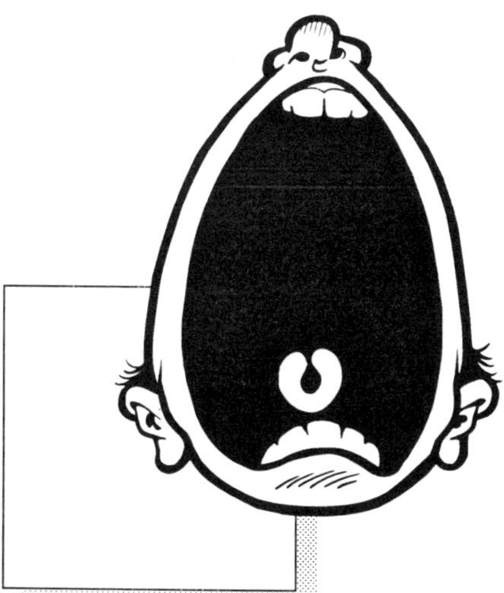

Read v19-22.

GLORY HUNTERS

See who's groaning here (v20a, 22)? And why (v20b)? After Adam and Eve rebelled, God put a curse on the world, and it's been trapped in a spiral of decay ever since.

• *What was God's purpose in doing this (v20b-21)?*

Read v23-27.

WAITING FOR GOD, OH!

• *Who else is groaning? And why (v23)?*

Catch how we can be sure all this will happen (23-24)? God's Spirit in us is like a first instalment: a taste of what things will be like once God finishes his work in us and a pledge that he will complete it.

• *What should our double attitude be while we wait (v23)?*

Eagerness and patience. Together? Yes! Ask God for them. And just as hope sustains us, so the Spirit helps us pray.

• *What's exciting about v26-27?*

Suffering before glory. But remembering v18 are you? Good!

For further study see the **OPTIONAL EXTRA** on page 61

ALL FOR SURE

Romans 8 v28-39

Hold on, hold on. Can we be *sure* of this future glory? Does God really keep hold of us? Even when life's tough?

Read Romans 8 v28-30.

ALL FOR GOOD

v28's smart! God's at work. In all things. For the good of his people, those called by him, who love him.

• *Is any situation of ours outside God's control?*

• *How do v29-30 help us understand how God works everything for the good of his children?*

Our 'good' is being made like Jesus: an ongoing process that's to be completed in glory. That's a more substantial 'good' than not missing buses or not catching colds, we think you'll agree.

Think why Paul says (in v30) we *have been* glorified. It's 'cos it's as good as done. As sure as God's other actions. So we know that God will finish what he has started in us.

Read v31-39.

GOD FOR US

Paul slaps down five questions. You'll see the answers are:

v31: 'nobody!'

v32: 'of course!'

v33: 'nobody!'

v34: 'nobody!'

v35: 'nobody! nothing!'

• *What is the point Paul is making?*

Whoever may be against us, God is greater, and he won't abandon us or let us go. Because he loves us.

• *Just how reassuring are v35-39?*

Whatever the opposition, danger or difficulties that tempt us to give up, nothing will separate us from Jesus' love, or from sharing his victory (v37). Paul's *convinced* about that (v38).

• *What things are you most afraid of?*

Add them to Paul's list in v38-39. And thank God that not even those things can stop his plans or his love for you.

Romans 9-16 is in the next issue. But that's Romans 1-8.

• *What in it will you make a point of thanking God for?*

For further study see the **OPTIONAL EXTRA** on page 61

PLOT ROT

Psalm 64

'Pssst! Go on, you'll get away with it!'

'Who's going to know it was you?'

'Even if you are found out, so what? Who cares?'

• Ever dished out advice like this? Or been given it?

Psalm 64 tells us what makes that advice good or bad... but you'll have to multiple-guess it to find out.

Read Psalm 64 v1-6.

Fire!

1. What's David doing (v1)?

a) asking for help; b) demanding his rights; c) complaining

He feared opponents plotting his (and others') downfall.

2. Why did he picture words as 'swords' and 'arrows' (v3)?

a) over-fertile imagination, pal; b) he's right; c) he's a poet

• What do words have the power to do?

3. What's the answer to the 'Who will see?' question (v5)?

a) definitely nobody; b) hopefully nobody; c) God

4. Is there ever a plan that will never be found out (v6)?

a) of course; b) but you're not telling us about it; c) no

• Why or why not?

• Is it possible even to deceive ourselves?

Catch David's conclusion about what we're really like (v6b)?

• How deep is the problem?

Read v7-10.

Backfire

5. What do such people (as in v6) overlook (v7)?

a) God's all-seeing; b) God hates wrong; c) God's got arrows

6. What's the inevitable result (v8-9)?

a) God will show his justice b) and be honoured c) by all

v10: precisely! God's people - those whose hearts are right - can trust God to act with justice: so those who do wrong won't - ultimately - get away with it. Thank God for what he's like!

• Why is this truth such a relief? Why is it a challenge, too?

* You want answers? You should have: c, a, abc, b, abc, c. But not in that order. Ha! You'll have to look in the psalm...

SUN BLESSED
Psalm 65

Harvest-time. Hurrah! Baked bean cans on the window-sills. School assembly about pumpkins. And singing! Yes, join in...

'All things trite and dutiful...'

Know the song? OK, our version's unfair, we agree. 'Cos harvest's a good thing from God. Psalm 65 says so. And more.

Read Psalm 65 v1-4.

BLEST

v1: 'in Zion' is a way of saying 'among God's people.'

v3: 'atoned' = 'paid the price for.'

v3: 'transgressions' = wrongdoing against God.

v4: 'temple': the sign of God's presence with his people.

• What big fact about God is David celebrating (v3-4)?

• How should this make God's people respond (v1)?

God forgives! Remarkable when you see the state we've got ourselves in (v3a). Are we able to change our own situation?

• What does it mean to you to be forgiven by God?

Read v5-9.

ZEST

• What aspects of God's character are these verses on about?

The Creator God rules his world (v7), saves his people (v5): remember some of God's mighty acts the Bible tells us about?

• What does v7 say he has power over?

• Why's it exciting we can rely on him for the future (v5b)?

Read v9-13.

'VEST

Ah, the harvest bit. Does harvest just happen automatically?

• Which verses here show how involved in it God is?

• How generous is God to his world (v9, 10, 11, 12... etc)?

All the more remarkable when you recall what we're like (v3).

That's psalm 65: God forgives, rescues, rules, provides. Now that's worth singing about. Isn't it?

SHOUT BOUT

Psalm 66

'... and first on Top of the Psalms, the one that's proved a real classic, it's been at no. 66 now for an incredible number of, er, centuries, yes, the one from the ever-popular singer/ songwriter David, here, tonight, live, it's *Come see, Come listen....*'

Thunderous studio applause. Let's hear it!

'Doo-wah, doo-wah, ah, doop-doop doo-wah

(it's the intro)...'

Read Psalm 66 v1-4.

YELL WELL

Try it (v1). Yes, you. Now.

Go on, right where you are. Shout. No, louder. SHOUT!

- *Why can't we help getting excited about God (v2-3)?*
- *Who was David issuing his invitation to (v1)?*

v5 on give us stuff to get us shouting and praising God.

'Chee-cha-cha, che-boom-shh, chee-boom

(etc, twiddly bit)...'

Read v5-15.

SEA SAW

v1 said all the earth should praise God because what he's done for his people has world-wide significance. Right?

- *What's v6 referring to?*
- *Why should everyone praise God, according to v7?*

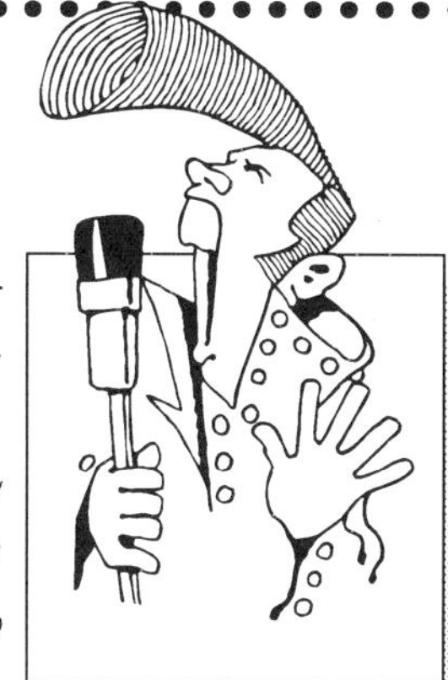

D & co, God's Old T people, knew God's great rescue (v8-9).

- *What did they also know to be from God (v11-12a)?*
- *But see what this led to (v10, 12b)? Superb!*

David says 'thanks God' for his care of his people (v13-15).

- *What do you need to remember about God's work in us, from these verses?*

Didididididididididididididididididididi (it's a final drumroll)...

Read v16-20.

HEAR HERE

- *What did David want God's people to remember (v16-18)?*
- *What did he know to be true about God (v19-20)?*

A great God! Not only did he hold back the sea for his people (v6)... he answers the prayers of one individual.

- *Can you shout about some of God's awesome deeds?*
- *Will you say what God has done for you, as v16b?*

SEVEN UP

Psalm 67

'A psalm with just 7 verses? And two of them are the same? Pah, it's a snack. We could gulp that down without blinking.

And without thinking. That's the danger. Please don't knock this psalm back so fast you fail to taste it. And what's the hurry anyway? Here, have a squizz at our Fizz Quiz...

Read Psalm 67.

WORLD FLAVOUR

The psalm is a prayer. OK, drink in these seven questions:

1. Who's doing the praying?

2. What for?

3. Is there a verse which seems to sum it up?

4. What's the psalm telling us about God?

5. What's it saying about his people?

6. What's it saying about his world?

7. Which verse particularly hits you? Why?

Hmm, more here that meets the eye, right?

v1 quotes the first words of a prayer that was said for God's Old T people (psst, it's Numbers 6 v22-27, if you must know). It's picture language, but beaut. Think what it would mean for God's people to have God's face 'shine' upon them.

• If that happened, what would follow? See the link with v2?

God's people would 'reflect' God to the world and make his rescue known to everybody. We reck v2 sums it up best.

• Then what would happen (v3-5, 6-7)?

You see, God chose a people for himself (that Old T Israelites) in order to make himself known to the *nations.*

• Grasped how Jesus is God's blessing to the world?

Thru' his people, God reaches those who don't know him. That's been his way all along.

• What are the implications of this for you?

• Why's it right to pray along the lines of v1-2, then?

RULING PASSION

1 Kings - introduction

If you think history is a snooze, press k.ing and surf into the age of Kings. Power struggles... epic battles... heart-breaking drama. And more. It's all here. And kicking.

The action's set in the united kingdom of Israel, the nation God chose to be his very own. Then civil war breaks out, and the kingdom splits in two - north and south.

To play Kings, you need to be able to spot the difference between a good and a bad king.

In Kings, a good king submits to God. Keeps his commands. Listens to God's spokesmen, the prophets. Leads God's people to do the same. And refuses to tolerate other gods.

David (in 1 & 2 Sam) was a good one. God promised to make his son king after him and sure enough, on strolled Solomon.

After a good start, Sol turned bad. And after him, things got worse among God's people. Mostly their kings were dire. God kept sending his prophets to show he was still in charge.

So, kick into Kings, this royal blockbuster:

- Observe God in the driving seat of history.
- Notice God's words carrying authority.
- Watch God not afraid to judge his people.
- See God keeping promises he made centuries before.
- Listen to God calling his people to love him back.
- Catch his concern for all peoples.
- And see how the shocking history of God's people under bad human kings points to the need for a King from God.

If you're a Christian, you know him personally. King Jesus. You won't find a better king than him - not among all the rulers of God's people you're about to meet...

* Kings comes in two parts: in this file we're going to play part one, which covers the period from around 970BC to 850BC.

DAD'S LADS

1 Kings 1

King David was old. And cold - he needed a human hot water bottle. Ad the lad, one of his sons (David had quite a few by different wives) exploited his dad's old age to stage a coup. But God wanted another of his lads on the throne.

Read 1 Kings 1 v1-10.

BAD AD

- *Why did David's grip on power seem to be slipping (v1-4)?*
- *What did Ad do (v5, 7, 9)? Why was this bad?*

Read v11-14.

NATH N' BATH

Nathan was God's spokesman, Bathsheba was one of David's wives and Sol's mum. ie, Sol and Ad were half-brothers. Er, danger, v12: Ad would be expected to wipe out all rivals.

- *So what did Nath arrange with Bath?*
- *Why was Sol the rightful king (v13)?*

Read v28-35.

DAVE SAVES

In v15-27, B & N spoke to David as planned.

- *How did David react (v28-30)?*
- *What kind of a king was David, then (v29-30)?*

See the ruse David dreamt up (v33-35): despite appearances, he hadn't lost his marbles. Oh no.

Read v41-53.

KIND KING

Big gig celebration when Sol got crowned (v36-40).

- *What news was reported back to Ad (v41-48)?*
- *How did Ad and co react (v49)? Why, do you think?*

You're a kind man, Sol (v52-53). And lucky lad, Ad.

God had said Sol would be king after David. God was in charge of the whole situation behind the scenes - and kept his word. As he always does. Thank God for what he's like. And think:

- *Why do you need to remember these truths about God?*

For further study see the **OPTIONAL EXTRA** on page 63

POWER SHOWER

1 Kings 2

Newly-crowned Sol got a firm grip on power. Not surprisingly. He'd got God on his side.

Read 1 Kings 2 v1-4.

LAST ORDERS

• *What was David's charge to his son (v2-4)?*

• *What was at stake (v3b, 4b)?*

See what God promised David (v4)? Think what his descendants would have to do to get the benefit of God's promise. v4's a big verse in Kings. Wait n' see, folks.

Read v5-12.

COMMAND FORCE

David didn't want to leave Sol with trouble-makers: pick out who was to get justice (v5-6), compassion (v7), and discipline (v8). See the reasons why, too?

• *How did David's advice help Sol (v12)?*

Now, we'll see exactly how Sol got a grip on power...

Read v13-25.

AD'S END

v22: Sol rightly took Ad's request as a bid for the throne (claiming priestly and military support, too). Outrageous.

• *Why did Sol need to get rid of Ad (v23-25)?*

Read v28-35 and v46.

DEATH ROW

Abiathar the priest, Joab the army leader, Shimei the rebel all got what God's justice called for.

Wham.

Trouble-makers were taken out. God controlled events so as to keep his promise to David and prosper Sol (v46).

• *Would he and his sons heed v4?*

Since God is that great, will you take a hint from v2-3, too?

For further study see the **OPTIONAL EXTRA** on page 63

Solomon. Ahh. Wisdom on legs. Well, wasn't he?

Read 1 Kings 3 v1-5.

Dream theme

Pick up the 4-point news summary (v1a,1b, 2, 3).

- *What kind of king was Sol at this point (v3)?*
- *Why was his move in v1a quite a massive mistake?*

'High places' (v2-3) were worship centres away from Jerusalem where people made sacrifices to God. Later on in Kings, people started worshipping false gods at these places (and that's idolatry). But at this point they're OK-ish, but not ideal.

- *Why were people using these high places (v2)?*

Read v6-15.

Thinking man's king

Just think: how would you have replied to God's offer in v5b?

- *What did Sol ask for (v9)? Why? (v7, 8, 9)?*

Think why God was pleased (v10). 

- *What does this teach us about the character of God?*

Read v16-28.

Baby talk

- *How would you have solved the dispute, then?*

- *How does this story show Sol's wisdom in practice?*

Read ch. 4 v20-21, 29-34.

Brain fame

Ch. 4 v1-28 shows Sol's wisdom in government.

- *What was life like for God's people with Sol in charge (v20)?*
- *Why was Sol a world genius (v29-30)?*

v34: superb. God was reaching the world thru' Sol.
But Sol was *far* from perfect: his decision to marry someone who wasn't one of God's people would later wreck his rule.

God was being *massively* generous to a flawed human king.Think why we must thank God for his generosity, too.

Hey! See 3 v26a: literally, it means 'her bowels grew hot.' Hmm. Funny place to feel compassion.

For further study see the **OPTIONAL EXTRA** on page 63

HOUSE WARMING

1 Kings 5 v1 - 8 v13

Under Sol, it was peace-time. Sol got on with building a house for God - the idea David had. But just see how he did it...

Read 1 Kings 5 v1-7.

Hi! I'm Hiram

• *Why could Solomon do what David couldn't (v3-4)?*

Skim thru' what this phenomenal, seven-year project involved:

Workforce (5 v13-16) Temple exterior (6 v2)

Interior design (6 v14-15) Inner room (6 v19-20)

Then they made the furniture and items to go in it (7 v13-51). Lavish, huh? Yes, but it was built by forced labour - among God's people (5 v13). Outrageous. And see how much longer Sol took over his own pad (7 v1)? That's offside, Sol.

But it must be time for the house-warming party, surely...

Read ch. 8 v1-9.

Hark! The ark!

(Uh? Cherubim, v6? What on earth...? OK, try the Opt Extra).

The 'ark' (v3) was a box. See what was in it (v9)?

ie, it was a reminder of God's agreement ('covenant') with his people. It symbolised God's holy presence with them. If they obeyed God, they'd stay in the land. But if not, not...

• *Where did the priests park the ark (v6)?*

• *Why's it significant it was put there?*

Read v10-13.

Grief, it's God

Learn God's reaction to the arrival of the ark (v10).

• *What are v10-11 telling us about God?*

• *What was Solomon's summary (v12-13)?*

The great God who is everywhere chose to share his presence with his people. He was near, yet he was far: there was no open access for an unholy people to a holy God.

We'll see how Sol prayed next. What about you?

• *What's the building of the temple taught you about God?*

For further study see the **OPTIONAL EXTRA** on page 64

HOUSE MASTER

1 Kings 8 v14-66

Shhh. It's speech time at Sol's Building Awards Ceremony.

Who's he going to thank for the temple?

His mum? The architects? 30,000 labourers? Himself?

Whom would he dedicate it to?

His dad? His Egyptian wife? The people? Those cherubim?

Let's listen in. Look, he's at the mike already. Shhh!

Read 1 Kings 8 v22-24.

I'D LIKE TO THANK...

- *Who's the only one to get applauded by Sol (v23)?*
- *Can you draw out the reasons why?*

Think what this tells us about God's character. Good, innit?

Read v27-30.

I PROPOSE A TOAST TO...

- *What left Sol totally gobsmacked (v27)?*

See the massive, undeserved favour Sol asked for (v30).

His plea 'hear from heaven...' gets repeated seven times in v31-53, with requests about the future of God's people: 'forgive... act... teach... deal... uphold... '

- *See God's concern even here for all people (v41-43)?*
- *How do v52-53 sum up Sol's request?*

Read v54-61.

I DEDICATE IT TO...

Sol's still praising God (v56). And rightly so.

- *What were his next three requests (v57, 58, 59)?*
- *What did he recognise that God expected of Israel (v61)?*

After the king-size 14-day dedication feast (v62-66), someone else spoke: a bit of a house warning... that's next.

Our God in heaven is incomparably great. And trustworthy. Sol knew that. Do you? Pray v61 will be true of you.

For further study see the **OPTIONAL EXTRA** on page 63

SPICE WHIRLED

1 Kings 9-10

Sol was at the height of his fame: Israel was experiencing a golden age. Join us, ladies and gents, as Sol met two special guests. One came to warn him, the other to test him...

Read 1 Kings 9 v1-9.

King's warning

- *How had God responded to Sol's prayer (v3)?*
- *What did he tell Sol to do (v4)?*

See the result if he obeyed God (v5). And if he didn't (v6-9).

- *How severe would God's punishment be?*
- *Would it be undeserved (v9)?*

v10-28 highlight Sol's business activities outside Jerusalem. And we're talking big biz, that is. See v14, 28?

Read ch. 10 v1-13.

Queen's visit

The world's first spice girl? Step forward Sheba Spice.

- *Why did she travel to Jerusalem?*
- *What did this queen want, really, really want (v1-2)?*

Looks like it was a sort of trade mission with all that stuff (v2).

- *What impressed her (v3-5)?*

Remember she was a foreigner - not one of God's people.

- *But what had Sol's wisdom taught her about God (v6-9)?*
- *What did she see that God expects of the king (v9)?*
- *Are you as eager to learn about God as she was?*

v14-29 describe Sol's splendour. Sample v23-25.

- *What's the key thing to remember about Sol's wisdom (v24)?*

Thank God for his gift of wisdom. Ask him to give you a greater insight into what he's like and what he expects of you.

For further study see the **OPTIONAL EXTRA** on page 63

Fatal Attraction

1 Kings 11

Sol had become the greatest king in the world.

Had he?

Well, he had bulging bagfuls of wisdom, gold and fame.

Big deal.

And he was given spices, ivory, weapons. And baboons.

Maybe. But just see what God would remember about him...

Read 1 King 11 v1-3.

Compromise

- *What did Sol do wrong (v1-2)?*

Let the scale of v3 sink in. *How* many?

Read v4-8.

Corruption

- *Who influenced whom (v4)? In what way (v5)?*
- *What's God's verdict on him (v6)?*
- *How far did Sol go in his idolatry (v7-8)?*

Read v9-13.

Catastrophe

- *Why had God every right to be angry (v9-10)?*
- *What would God do (v11)? And not do (v12-13)?*

In v14-25, the judgment began. See the opening of v14 &23?

Peace was shattered: Sol began to get hassle from enemies.

Read v26-40.

Challenger

Not only enemies, now it's oppo from one of God's people.

- *What did Ahijah the prophet predict about Jeroboam here?*
- *How would God still keep his promises (v36, 39)?*

Read v41-43.

Conclusion

Sol had blemishes all along. Disobedience led to disaster.

- *What has ch. 11 whacked home to you about God?*

Pray you'll keep going in the Christian life.

For further study see the **OPTIONAL EXTRA** on page 64

Side splitting

1 Kings 12

Duh. Sol's son Rehoboam didn't inherit his dad's wisdom. His stupidity split Sol's kingdom in two.

Duh again. Then that bloke called Jeroboam (11 v26, yeah?) widened that split into a whopping great yawning chasm.

The surprise wasn't just that God knew exactly what was going on. It was that the outcome was fully part of his plan.

Read 1 Kings 12 v1-11.

Jerobjective

After Sol's death, Jerob was back in town. And he led the delegation of Israelites to Rehob, Sol's son - the new king.

• *What did they want (v4)?*

ie, less forced labour, less taxes and less army service, please.

Rehob took advice. But from the wrong people.

Read v12-24.

Rehobellion

• *Why was Rehob stupid to listen to his mates (v12-15)?*

• *But what was God up to in all this (v15)?*

So the Israelites told Rehob to take a hike (v15-17) - and the kingdom split in two (just as God had said):

Judah: location: south; capital: Jerusalem; king: Rehob.

Israel: location: north; capital: Shechem (at first); king: Jerob.

In chs. 12-22, the action switches between north and south.

Read v25-33.

Jerobnoxious

Count how many times (in v25-33) Jerob went badly wrong. (Then try our answers in the Opt Ex.)

• *Why did Jerob make the golden calves (v26-30)?*

• *Why was Jerob seriously bad news (v31-33)?*

Sol's sin led to downright disaster: a split kingdom among God's own people and Israel worshipping false gods.

Crisis? It was only just beginning. More next...

You can't play games with God. Learnt that yourself?

For further study see the **OPTIONAL EXTRA** on page 64

Speak and Destroy

1 Kings 13-14

Jerob, king of Israel, was Mr Big Guns. Loaded with power. But he soon found himself outgunned by words from God. Watch three direct hits blow him and his rule to bits...

Read 1 Kings 13 v1-10.

Altar ego

The missile carrier was an obscure prophet from the south - the man of God from Judah (v1), sent by God. He homed in on king Jerob while he worshipped the golden calf at Bethel.

Hit 1: see the launch (v1-3). And the damage (v4-5).

• *How did this incident show the power of God's word?*

• *How much did it change Jerob?*

v7-10: a meal with Jerob, one under God's judgment? No, ta.

v11-32: God told the man of God to go straight back home - but a northern prophet conned him into disobeying God.

Hit 2: what happened (read v23-26)?

• *What should the man of God have done first off (v26a)?*

• *How much did this change Jerob (read v33-34)?*

Read ch. 14 v1-18.

Ill will

Abijah. Ahijah. It's a name nightmare. Don't nurdle 'em up. Maybe Jerob thought he'd get a nice prediction from Ahijah, like he did before (11 v31). Fat chance.

• *What did Ahijah tell Mrs Jerob (v7-11)?*

Hit 3: dung-burningly direct judgment (v10).

• *Which phrases show how definite God's judgment was?*

• *What would happen as a result of Jerob's sin (v14-16)?*

Read v21-24.

Sin son

The action switches to Judah: to Sol's son, king Rehob.

• *Why was he woefully bad news, too (v22-24)?*

God has spoken. You've got it in print in front of you.

And he punishes those who fail to take his word seriously.

• *How do chs. 13-14 urge us to obey God? Will you?*

For further study see the **OPTIONAL EXTRA** on page 65

Go it, Poet

1 Kings 15-16

We've just dug up a rare poem on 1 Kings. Never published before, we present it below, line by line, limerick-style. Rehob's son, Abijah, was as bad as his dad. But then a good king burst onto the southern scene. Enjoy the poetry!

Read 1 Kings 15 v9-15.

There once was a king called Ace,
Who walked with God step by pace...

• *What was ace about Asa (v11-13)?*

But was that the full story (v14)? Remember the high places were where people worshipped false gods.
Back in Israel, meanwhile, a thug called Baasha gained power:

Read v25-32.

While Bash used his sword...

• *What did Bash's carnage (v29-30) demonstrate (v29b)?*

The word of God came true. God was still in charge of these events even tho' his kings were appallingly brutal.

Read ch. 16 v1-6.

And, by God got floored...

See what would land in Bash's plate - and why (v2-4)?
It happened, as God said (v12). Then, three kings after Bash, a nasty piece of work called Ahab became Israel's king no. 7:

Read v29-34.

King Ahab proved a God-less disgrace.

• *What was Ahab's attitude to disobeying God (v30-31)?*
• *Why was his marriage to Jezebel a disastrous move (v31)?*

Baal (pronounce it how you like) was a revolting nature god.
• *How devoted was Ahab to Baal (v32)?*
• *In what way was Ahab well out of order (v33)?*

But God was still in charge. Ahab would'nt get off lightly.

Now forget the poem.
Think what today's Bible slice should remind you about God - and his purposes for his people.

For further study see the **OPTIONAL EXTRA** on page 65

JAW JAH JAR

1 Kings 17

Israel sunk to an all-time low under Ahab. So God sent his spokesman, Elijah (to pronounce it, say 'hello' with an Aussie accent and add 'jar'). The Elijah v Ahab showdown showed God was in charge. Follow our big fight mini-commentary...

Read 1 Kings 17 v1-6.

OI!

'Powerful early flurry of punches from Elijah. He's carrying out his prophet's job: reinforcing Gods' covenant. Ahab's hit hard right on the chin - he's going to face the consequences of disobeying God: famine, as God had warned his people.'

- *How did Elijah describe God to Ahab (v1)? See his point?*
- *How did Elijah describe himself?*
- *In what way would God show Ahab who's boss?*

'Saved by the bell. Then long gap between rounds. Elijah's given some training.'

Read v7-16.

OIL!

Sidon (v9) was where Jezebel, Ahab's wife came from. God (he's always been concerned to reach all peoples) sent Elijah into foreign territory - where Baal was worshipped.

'It would be good for his fitness, great practice, shape him up to rely on God...'

- *What miracle did God do thru' Elijah there (v16)?*
- *What does it remind us about God?*

God was in charge outside Israel as well as in.

Read v17-24.

OIK!

'Crisis in training... but the experience taught Elijah a lesson. And the woman, too, judging by the interview she gave the press.'

- *How did Elijah respond to the crisis (v20)?*
- *Which 3 verses show who's responsible for the miracle?*

See how the widow reacted (v24)? Remember, she wasn't an Israelite, one of God's people. Her lot worshipped Baal.

- *But what has she realised about God's word?*

Thank God that his word is both true and powerful.

'And wait for Elijah v Ahab round two.'

For further study see the **OPTIONAL EXTRA** on page 65

HIGH NOON AT OK CARMEL

1 Kings 18 v1-29

The big fight's back on. This next bit's a highpoint of 1 Kings. Some people say it's their fave bit of the whole Old T. Well, we'll take two pages over it. Take your seat!

Read 1 Kings 18 v1-15.

OB JOB

v1: drought's dragged on - God's ongoing judgment against Ahab and the people of God for their disobedience.

• *But now what was about to happen (v1)?*

• *What was Elijah told to do?*

Explain why the royal official Ob was a good lad (v3-4).

• *Why was he thrown into a tizzy (v9-12, 14)?*

Noticed Ahab's response to the famine (v5)?
No trust in God, mere self-reliance. The bozo.

Read v16-24.

CARMEL CRUNCH

• *Why was Ahab the real 'troubler of Israel' (v17-18)?*

• *What challenge did Elijah throw down to Ahab (v22-24)?*

See the crisis among God's people (v21)?

• *What made their indecision outrageous?*

• *Why is this moment such a crunchpoint (v21-22)?*

Elijah's job was to call God's people to obey him.
But would they turn back to God? Or was it too late for that?

Read v25-29.

BAAL FAILS

Smell the blood and sweat. Hear the chants. Watch the day-long gruesome frenzy. And chortle at Elijah's sarcasm (v27).

• *Why was Baal a total loser (v29)?*

Elijah then called God's people together. But his role wasn't just to outdo the Baal prophets in arranging a stunt...

* Wait for the Opt Extra! Bag it after the next page, please.

FIRE PROOF

1 Kings 18 v30-46

Big fight, part two. Pumped up for it?

Read v30-37.

ALTAR CALL

Glue your eyes to v30-32, 36-37: what was Elijah up to?

The repair job (v30), the 12 stones (v31), the altar 'in the name of the LORD' (v32), the time of sacrifice (v36), his prayer that God would change his people's hearts (v37) ...

Elijah wanted God's people to remember what God was like. To recall that God would forgive his people's disobedience - by means of sacrifice. To come back to him, heart and soul.

v33-35: nice touch, mate. Using up water, gallons of it - in a drought. He's trusting God not only for fire, but rain.

• *What things did Elijah calmly ask God to do (v36-37)?*

Read v37-46.

DROUGHT OUT

Elijah's prayer (v37) was answered a.s.a.p.

• *What was God's response - out of a cloudless sky (v38)?*

• *And the people's (v39)?*

v40: unnecessary violence? Oh no. Deserved. They'd turned God's people against him.

• *What did God do for Israel once all this was over (v45)?*

Once his people's sin had been taken away by sacrifice, God gave rain once more. In some style, too (v45).

The Carmel contest showed Baal was no god at all. And it showed the God of Israel had power. And was again prepared to forgive his people - thru' sacrifice.

Thank God that he's the one and only.
Pray that you and your friends would realise that.
And thank God for what he's like.

For further study see the **OPTIONAL EXTRA** on page 66

FEEL IT BURN

1 Kings 19

After the big burn-out on Carmel, it was now Elijah's turn. To get burned out, that is. How would God deal with him?

a) 'oi, Elijah, keep going' *b) 'right, you're fired' (ha!)*

c) 'look, you're not that tired' *d) 'OK, tell me all about it'*

e) 'right, let's take breather' *f) 'I told you so'*

Let's find out...

Read 1 Kings 19 v1-9a.

CRASH OUT

Jez was undaunted by God's display of power at Carmel.

- *What was her threat (v2)? Why, do you think?*
- *Was Elijah's reaction (v3) right, wrong, or fair enough?*

Elijah showed outsize courage on Carmel. But, instead of trusting God again, he scarpered, shattered by it all (v5).

- *What did he say to God (v4)?*
- *What's great about the way God looked after him (v5-9)?*

Read v9b-18.

STAKE OUT

Elijah went *miles* to Horeb (where God gave his people his the 10 Commandments). Think why Elijah went there.

- *But what did God think of his move (v9b)?*
- *What were Elijah's three reasons for running off (v10)?*

God's people were in a dire state (v10): in *opposition* to God.

- *Surprisingly, how did God show himself to Elijah (v12)?*

God spoke in a whisper. He speaks *words* - so no confusion. And he gave Elijah a new task - appointing kings to carry out a massacre: God's judgment against his people.

- *But how did he also rebuke and reassure Elijah (v18)?*

Read v19-21.

STEP OUT

- *What was Elisha doing when Elijah found him (v19)?*
- *How did he make a clean break with his farming life (v21)?*

God's people were sliding towards his no-mess judgment. But remember as well today how God cares for those who serve him - in our human weakness.

For further study see the **OPTIONAL EXTRA** on page 66

BIG BEN'S HIGH NOON

1 Kings 20

Flak jacket time: the king of Aram (modern Syria) was about to wade in on Israel's capital, Samaria.

But he underestimated Israel's God.

The battle was also a last test for Ahab. Would he change?.

Read 1 Kings 20 v1-4.

WHO'S BEN HAD?

See what B-H demanded (v2)?

Ahab gave in (v4), then changed his mind. Big Ben got ready.

Read v13-30.

BEN WELL BEAT

- *What did God's prophet promise Ahab (v13)?*

True to form, God brought victory: with unusual tactics (v19), odd timing (v16) and inexperienced fighters (v15).

- *What mistake did the Syrians then make (v23)?*
- *What would God do to them - and why (v28)?*

God's not just a local god. He's the God of everywhere.

Think: how are you tempted to under-estimate God?

Read v31-34.

BEN LET OFF

- *Despite a God-given victory, what did Ahab do (v34)?*

ie, he struck a deal with the guy who'd just tried to obliterate God's people Israel. Bonehead! What should he have done?

Read v35-43.

BEN CAUGHT

- *Great sketch, but what was its point (v42)?*
- *What would God do to Ahab? Remember why?*

Ahab had blown it. God, in his long-suffering, could wait no more. Ahab had brought his own punishment on his head.

- *What's your response to God from this chapter?*

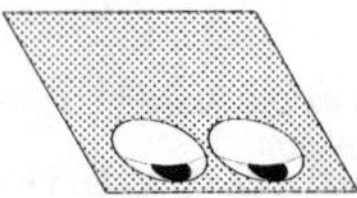

For further study see the **OPTIONAL EXTRA** on page 67

NAB THY NEIGHBOUR

1 Kings 21

The Ahab-Jezebel double act sunk to new low. In the next story, we get cowardice, theft, murder and one of the most grumpy, infantile, self-centred tantrums in history.
Oh, and Ahab does something totally out of character...

Read 1 Kings 21 v1-16.

NAB NABBED

• *What did Ahab hanker after (v1-2)?*

A fair offer? Maybe, but Nab was far more honourable (v3). Look at Ahab's crashing immaturity (v4). Unbelievable.

• *Who wore the trousers in Ahab's pad (v5-7)?*

• *What did Ahab allow to happen (v8-14)?*

Read v17-28.

AHA AHAB!

• *What did God think of their action (v17-19)?*

• *What does this teach us about the character of God?*

Bag what God would do to Ahab (v20-22). And why (v25-26).

• *And what about Jezebel (v23)?*

See what made God decide not to destroy Ahab's family during his lifetime (v28-29).

• *What does that say to you about the character of God?*

Hold on. God showed incredible kindness to Ahab, the worst king in Israel's history... but his patience finally ran out. Next!

Jot down what ch. 21 has to teach us about God:
ie, what's his attitude to his people? And his people's sin?

• *How will this make you pray?*

For further study see the **OPTIONAL EXTRA** on page 67

WAR OF WORDS
1 Kings 22

Q. What's the difference between a true spokesman of God and a false one? **A.** *(no, you answer it)*

Q. What's the difference between a good king over God's people and a duff one? **A.** *(yes, your turn again)*

Stumped? Well, ch. 22 has answers. Come and spot the diffs...

Read 1 Kings 22 v1-9.

RG bargy

- *What did Jehosh and Ahab plan jointly (v3-4)?*
- *But how was Jehosh different from Ahab (v5)?*
- *Had Ahab changed his attitude to God much (v8)?*

TV cameras everywhere, the nation waiting... for mighty Mick.

Read v10-28.

M v people

Mickey-take at the mike: Mick strung Ahab along (v15) - before delivering his devastating prediction (v17): Ahab's death and the break-up of the army.

- *How does this story show Mick's courage?*

That means... a Christian who wants to be true to the Bible will sometimes have to say truths that people won't like.

- *How is Mick a challenge to you?*

Read v29-40.

D day

- *How did the word of God come true (v34, 35, 37-38)?*

Now meet Ahab's boy (see v51-53). Like father, like son, eh? There 1 Kings stops. Just like that. Leaving us gasping to know how this period in the story of God's people would end. (Look out for 2 Kings with the Ichthus File. Next issue!)

1 Kings has shown us a lot of kings. And a lot of prophets.

- *What has the book rammed home to you about God?*
- *How should it change your attitude to God's words?*

* Able to answer the two opening questions now? Hope so. Thanks for trucking thru' 1 Kings with us. Well done!

For further study see the **OPTIONAL EXTRA** on page 67

FOLLOW THE LEADER

Psalm 68 v1-20

Ever sung another country's national anthem? It's bizarre. Doesn't feel right. Like wearing someone else's wellies. You don't know the words, the tune, the history...

But today, please try. Sing along to a psalm that may start off feeling like all sort-of unfamiliar. But as you sing along, you should just find stuff you can echo too. Echo, too. This psalm's an Old T praise march. Follow the band leader!

Read Psalm 68 v1-3.

Warm up!

The psalm could refer to the time when the ark of God (which symbolized the actual presence of God among his people) was brought back to Jerusalem (like the 2 Sam 6 party).

• What did it make David pray (v1-3)?

• What did he know to be true about God here?

Read v4-10.

They're off!

• What were David's orders (v4)?

• Why should God's people join in celebrating God (v4b-6)?

See the works of God that David's recalling: the rescue from Egypt (v6b), his leading thru' the desert (v7) to Canaan (v10). And Sinai (v8b) - the time God drew close to his people and gave them the 10 Commandments - his covenant with them.

• What stands out about God in these verses?

Read v11-14.

Sing along!

It's the crowd shouting all sorts of different chants.

• What have they recognised about God?

• What did it mean for them to be part of the people of God?

Read v15-20.

Nearly there!

v15: nice scenery nearby, sure, but nothing compared to being the place where God dwelt on earth. Wow!

v17: 'sanctuary' = the special place where the ark of God would be kept (and so where God's presence was).

• Just how great is God then (v19-20)?

• Stuff you can echo here?

Keep on following. More next!

Tune Army

Psalm 68 v21-35

OK, keep belting out the tunes. You're doing mighty fine.

Read Psalm 68 v21-23.

Little bit further

• *What will happen to those who defy God (v21)?*

• *Is there anywhere they can escape from God (v22)?*

And victory will be God's gift to his people (v23). Yes!

• *Remember what sort of God we're dealing with?*

Read v24-27.

Here we are!

Maybe at this point the procession with the ark of God has reached the sanctuary place in Jerusalem.

And all of God's people (v27) were involved in the jubilation.

Today God lives among his people by his Spirit.

• *What's incredible about that?*

Read v28-31.

Now then

• *Why could David be confident of God's future help (v28)?*

• *What did he pray would happen (v29, 30, 31)?*

v30: the 'beast' might = Egypt and the 'bulls' = surrounding countries. David envisaged (v31) a time when all nations would recognise the rule of God. One day they will!

Read v32-35.

Chorus again!

God not only rules his world. He draws near to his people. The awesome presence of God with them.

• *Whom should we call to worship God (v32)? Why (v33-35)?*

• *Will you share with your friends your enthusiasm for God?*

And before you go...

Now we today live after Jesus came.

• *How much more have God's people now got to shout about?*

• *What words will you use to praise God?*

(More? On v18, see Eph 4 v7-18. It's all fulfilled in Jesus!)

SINKING MAN'S PSALM

Psalm 69 v1-21

One of the best things about the psalms is the chance they give us to sit on someone's shoulder and listen as they pray.

Do that now with David (also known here as Percy Cute. Ed). He's having a tough time. In fact, it's getting to him deep down.
And he can't just shrug it off and keep trucking...

Read Psalm 69 v1-6.

BLAMED

• *What state was David in (v1-2)?*
• *How do the three pictures (v1a. 2a, 2b) sum it up?*

He'd found zero human help. Cheers, guys (v3).
• *What was it that drove him under (v4)?*
• *What was his worry for the rest of God's people?*

Read v7-12.

SHAMED

More honest talking to God about his desperadoes.
• *What was he having to face (v7, 9b, 10b, 11b, 12)?*
• *From whom (v8, 9b, 12)?*

Catch v9: it's his desire to please God that sparked all this.
Hey. Pause for a moment here:
• *Anything in the psalm so far that you relate to?*
• *Anything in the way he talks to God worth imitating?*
• *Anything about taking flak for living God's way?*

Read v13-21.

CLAIMED

As well as the jeers, people were even slipping poison into his supper (v21). Seconds? Er, no thanks. But had David given up altogether? Just resigned himself to life like this?
• *What was he still sure of (v13b, 16)?*

• *What did this make him do (v13a, 14-15, 16-18)?*

David prayed remembering what God is like. He knew God to be generous and trustworthy. And that shaped his prayers.
• *Take the hint, will you?*

Part two on the next page. Join us there.

PRAYING MAN, 'TIS

Psalm 69 v22-36

Keep praying David. Or Percy. We're still sitting on your shoulder. And still listening.

Make sure you are. 'Cos this next prayer seems a shocker.

Read Psalm 69 v22-28.

SMASH 'EM!

Eeek. Watch how David's requests build up, up, up to v28.

• *What was David actually praying for?*

Catch the links with David's own situation. eg:

He got poisonous food (v21) ... so may his enemies (v22).

Similarly, see how these pairs of verses connect (er, maybe):

v4 with v24 v8 with v25 v10-12 with v27

Can you imagine praying like this? Not without an awful dose of self-seeking revenge. But David clearly recognised God is just: ultimately he'll punish all who defy him.

• *How will knowing God's justice change the way you pray?*

Read v29-36.

SMASHING!

• *How could he switch so fast from what he said in v29 to what he said in v30?*

• *What was he still thoroughly sure of (v29b)?*

See how he put it in v33: 'The LORD hears the needy'.

• *How much do you believe this?*

• *Since that's true (v33), what should result (v34)?*

David was confident again of God's faithfulness to his people. In this psalm, he began praying in desperation. But he ended by praising God and calmly trusting him for the future.

• *What brought about this change?*

Think what this psalm has got to teach us. And then take those truths into your prayer time.

Won't you?

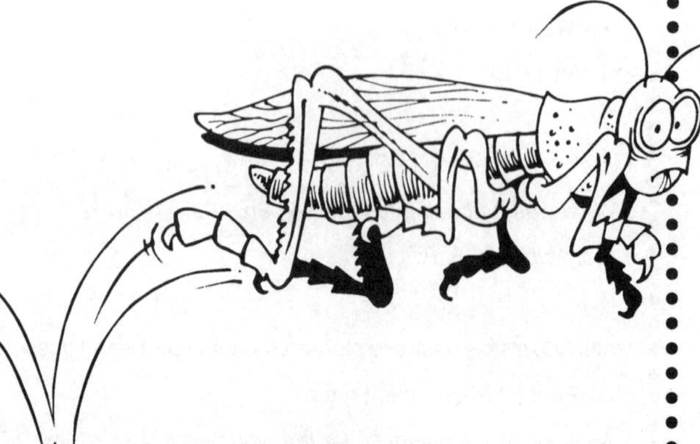

You've finished the study, but want to know more? Or perhaps you've an urge to stretch yourself further. Then the Optional Extra pages are for you. They're optional. And they're ... yes, you get the idea.

They provide additional questions, topics and ideas and often lead to other related passages in the Bible. You'll find they zing home quite strongly what it all means for you and me.

DEAR MR BOOKSHOP MANAGER

I'd like to order regular copies of *The Ichthus File* - daily Bible reading notes. Please order me up a regular copy, and I promise I'll call in and pick 'em up. I'll even pay for them!

Name .... Tel ....

Address ....

.... postcode ....

Note to Bookseller:
The Ichthus File is published by St Matthias Press, P.O.Box 665, London SW20 8RL. Call 0181-947 5686 to order, or fax through on 0181-944 7091.

DEAR ICHTHUS FILE TEAM

I'd like to order regular copies of *The Ichthus File* - deliver them straight to my door or I'll explode.

Name .... Tel ....

Address ....

....

Postcode .... Last issue received: ......

Make cheques payable to *St Matthias Press* and send to: P.O.Box 665, London SW20 8RL.

OR PAY BY CREDIT CARD:

Card no .... Expiry date ....

Name on card ....

Billing Address (if different from above) ....

....

....

DEAR YOUTH GROUP LEADER

What do you mean you've never heard of the Ichthus File? Call the boys on 0181-947-5686 to talk about getting the rest of your group on the best Bible notes around...

WHAT DO I DO NEXT?

You want more? *The Ichthus File* comes out every two months, with enough Bible input and encouragement to keep you going. You can buy back issues at your local bookshop, or by dialling 0181-947 5686 with a credit card handy. If you want to subscribe, we suggest the following alternatives:

1. Snip out the box top right and give it to your local Christian bookshop. They'll order it in for you every issue so that you can pop in and buy it from them. Or else stick a brick through the window and nick it. On second thoughts...

2. Carve out the middle box and get your Mum/Dad/Guardian/Zookeeper to write out a cheque, or fill in the credit card details. We'll send you the next six issues (one every two months) entirely for free. No only kidding - for £12.50 - you save £2.50 and it's delivered hot and steaming with a radiation warning on the packet straight to your door. Alternatively, you could get hold of a credit card and ring us up on 0181-947 5686 to order it. On third thoughts, ask their permission first.

3. Slice off the bottom box and hand it to your youth club leader - get him to arrange for you and others in the group to get regular copies, and you could all come away with a major cash bonus... it may do him/her a lot of good as well.

Optional extra

ROMANS 1-8

OPEN TO OFFER

Welcome to the RDDDC.

The **R**omans **D**igging **D**eliciously **D**eeper **C**rew. Here goes! So, who started the church at Rome? Dunno. It might just have been those mentioned in Acts 2 v10: visitors from Rome who were in Jerusalem at Pentecost. Could be!

v1: this letter's from Paul, *the apostle*. There are no apostles today. Those men were witnesses to Jesus' resurrection and specially chosen by him to pass on his truth. They speak with Christ's authority. This makes Romans more than an interesting 1st century letter. It's the word of God, no less.

Would you say that the Old Testament is important?

- *Why should we, according to v2?*

Jesus has risen from the dead (v4). Now read that again.

- *Why should this truth revolutionise our lives?*

Can we accept Jesus' rescue but not change how we live?
Can we accept him as Saviour, but not as Lord?

- *Why not? How do v4-5 help you?*
- *Are you trusting Jesus and obeying him?*

v5: 'for his name's sake'. Take a hint here:

- *What above all motivated Paul to share the gospel?*

Are you a Christian? You belong to Jesus Christ (v6).

- *What's brilliant about that, then?*

ROAM SWEET ROME

v8: faith is taking God at his word. Taken that in yourself?

v11: it's not clear what the 'gift' might be - but Paul's aim would be to see their needs and then build them up as Christians.

- *How serious was Paul about his gospel work (v9)?*
- *What's worth imitating about his prayer (v10)?*

v16: 'the gospel is the *power* of God...'

- *How have you known this to be true?*
- *Why should we be so thankful to God for the gospel (v17)?*

Make a list of your non-Christian friends and family.
Ever think some of them aren't 'at the right stage' for you to talk about the gospel with them? Or don't even need it?

- *What would Paul say to such questions?*
- *So, how will you now make progress with those friends?*

Jesus foresaw that his followers might be ashamed of him - but said we'd every reason not to be.
Grab Mark 8 v38 and 2 Tim 1 v8, 12. Feel convicted? Then admit that to God and ask him to help you stick by the gospel.

v16b: why Jews first? Simply 'cos God chose them as his Old T people. They ought to be the first to turn to Jesus! See how Paul put it in Acts 13 v44-48.

v15: chew over why Paul thinks it important to teach this great gospel to *Christians,* too. Why is he right to do so?

Optional extra

TRAMPLING TRUTH

Paul's proof that all need God's salvation (1 v16) starts with:

1. The depraved Gentile (non-Jewish) world, 1 v18-32; then

2. Proud, 'holier-than-thou' types (2 v1-16);

3. Self-confident Jews (2 v17 - 3 v8);

4. Paul's summary: absolutely everybody (3 v9-20).

Using v18-32, tell us what you think (and why) of these quotes:

'We can't plead innocence 'cos we can't plead ignorance.'

'Grasp God's anger before you grasp God's love.'

'People reject Jesus because they think they don't need him - or they're unwilling to admit it.'

'Christians must not be embarrassed about the wrath of God.'

'Idolatry inevitably leads to immorality.'

Which verses in 18-32 show sin is:

a) deliberate b) inexcusable?

• *Have you realised this about yourself?*

v26-27: er, what's Paul saying about homosexual behaviour?

1. It displeases God: since this conduct is a result of God's wrath ('God gave them over...'), it must do so.

2. It's against his created order: 'unnatural' here must mean against the way God created us.

Need to check that? See Gen 1 v27-28, 2 v24, Matt 19 v4-6.

v20: God's creation reveals him and his power to everyone.

• *See how Psalm 19 v1-6 puts it?*

Now whistle up John 1 v1, 14, 18.

• *How does Jesus reveal God to us far more fully?*

INESCAPABLE, INEXCUSABLE

v1: the old gag that 'when you point a finger at someone else, you've got three pointing back at yourself' is downright true.

• *How do you fall into the trap of think of setting incredibly high standards for others, but low ones for yourself?*

• *When you last criticised someone else, how much of that criticism could have been directed at you?*

v5: 'the day of God's wrath'. Don't treat this lightly.

• *How should it affect your behaviour now?*

v6: 'Hang on! Paul said we're rescued by faith in Jesus (1 v16), not by doing good. Explain this one!'

Sure, we're saved by faith, but here Paul's talking about judgment. And saying judgment will be on our deeds - 'cos that's the *public* evidence of our faith in Jesus. What a person *does* is the clue to what he *is*. Chew on that.

v7-8: the contrast's between those who seek (God's) glory and his honour and life with him, and those who are utterly self-seeking, reject the truth and follow evil.

v16: 'secrets': Paul's not talking about surprise birthday party plans. No, it's wrong motives, fantasies, thoughts we hide.

• *What secrets will you confess to God and leave behind?*

v16b: 'as my gospel...' ie, we won't understand God's love till we've grasped it rescues us from God's coming judgment. Judgment's a major theme of the gospel, folks. Let's face it.

Optional extra

SHAKEY JAKEY

v25: on circ., see Gen 17 v9-14, Deut 10 v16, 30 v6.

Catch the argument here:
v25: circ. minus obedience = uncirc. (ie, just like Gentiles).
v26: uncirc. plus obedience = circ (ie, like God's people).
See, it's obedience that comes from faith (1 v5) that God's concerned to see in his people. And still is.

3 v1-8 is like Paul having a debate with someone such as Jake the Jew. Jake has 4 objections to Paul's teaching:
a) 'Your teaching, Paul, insults God's covenant by saying there's no advantage in being a Jew' (v1).

b) 'It suggests God's ability to keep his promises depends on whether his people keep them' (v3).

c) 'If you say the more sinful we are, the greater the gospel seems to be, then that's like saying our being sinful benefits God. So God would then be unjust to punish us' (v5).

d) 'So you're saying our sinfulness is actually doing God a favour...' (v7-8a).
• *Can you work out Paul's answers (v2, 4, 6, 8b)?*

It's almost as if he doesn't reply to the objections. He just *asserts* what's true about God. As if to say: 'there's no point arguing here. These are the truths about God, like it or not.'

Well done for digging deep into this. Worth it, huh?

NO WIN, NO-ONE

v10-18: why quote so hugely from the Old T? Probably...
a) so the Gentile Christians would see clearly the truth of human sin and God's judgment from the Old T;
b) so any Jewish Christian would see that the Jews too were included in this verdict.

And in case one of them might reply and say: 'Ah yes, but all those verses are talking about Gentiles, not us Jews', Paul whacks in v19a: 'No, they're not, they're about you Jews.'

Catch the flow of Paul's thought:
1 v20: Gentiles are without excuse before God;
2 v1: so are any who think they're morally superior;
3 v9, 19: so are Jews. ie, everybody's without excuse.

Think what excuses we make to pretend we're OK with God.
'I'm not as bad as a criminal.'
'I can't help my own human nature. I was born this way.'
'I can't really be expected to keep God's perfect standards.'
'I do some pretty good things which God must like.'
• *Do you hide behind any of these?*
• *Can you think of any others?*
• *How does Romans 1-3 shoot down all these excuses?*

All around us are people who know enough of God to make their rejection of him totally inexcusable.
• *Where does v19's verdict leave your non-Christian friends?*
• *What should it make us Christians do?*

Optional extra

CROSS CHANNEL

v21: in contrast to our unrighteousness and stupid claims of self-righteousness... here's God's free gift of righteousness. Every other religion teaches self-salvation: 'do this... and you'll be 'in' with God.'

• *Now see why the gospel is called good news?*

Catch v21b again. Was this initiative God's afterthought - a sort-of mopping-up operation after his world had gone wrong?

• *So what are we learning about his plan?*

Incredible, huh? The cross wasn't Emergency Plan B, as if God was caught by surprise by our rejection of him. No, it was all part of his plan, announced in advance in the Old T.

• *How great does this make God?*

v24: on redemption, see Lev 25 v47-55, Ex 15 v13, Is 43 v1.

• *How does this help explain the redemption Jesus brought?*

'God himself gave himself to save us from himself.' Wow.

• *Can you explain that using 3 v21-26?*

ABRAHAM LINK ON

OK, so why does Paul decide to crack on about Abraham?

• *How might this help the Gentile Christians in Rome to grasp that they were now true members of God's people?*

• *How might it help any Jewish Christian to see that Paul's gospel of justification by faith wasn't a heretical novelty?*

Gobble Genesis 15 v1-6 to see how Abe showed faith.

v5: 'the man who does not work...' doesn't mean 'the fat slob who won't get a job' but 'whoever recognises he can't get right with God by his own efforts.'

v5b: God justifying the wicked: but he can't just *forget* sin!

• *Remembering 3 v24-26 are you?*

v7-8: from Ps 32. ie, when we're justified, God says he will never count our sins against us. Do you believe this?

• *What effect might it have on your behaviour as a Christian?*

CREDIT, NOTE

Trace the idea of Abraham as a father: v1, 11-12, 16-17, 18.

Bag Hebrews 11 v8, 9, 11, 17-19. And pick out the four occasions in which Abe's remembered for his faith in God.

• *Will you, like him, fully trust God's promises?*

• *Why's it more reasonable for us to trust God?*

v17b: eg, in creation, God called forth a world out of *nothing.*

'Faith looks at the problems in the light of the promises.'

• *See that in Abraham (v18): 'against hope... in hope'?*

• *How will you apply this principle to yourself right now?*

In the Bible, a person's considered to have saving faith when they know the truth necessary to save them, submit to it, rely on it and trust in Jesus. Does this describe you?

Look out for God's promises in the Bible. And believe them!

Optional extra

THE GOODY BAG

Fizzing stuff, Romans. Wouldn't you agree? Yeah boy howdy.

• *What do you need to remember so far?*

v3: Christians should be happy when they suffer, apparently.

• *Do you think this means whenever we suffer (like if you cut your foot) or only certain types of suffering?*

• *What is the point of our sufferings?*

• *Does this make the idea of rejoicing when we suffer for God seem easier to accept?*

Look up 1 Peter 4 v12-19. See v15? Think of some situations where you might suffer because of the name of Christ.

• *Is it easy to rejoice about these?*

v6-8: zip out at least 3 amazing truths here abut God's love.

Use 5 v1-11 to answer:

• *Why should Christians be the most positive people out?*

• *How do you shape up now? And what if life gets tougher?*

PEOPLEWATCH

v12's unfinished, but v18b sort of finishes it. Same idea, yeah?

v12c: it's not just that we copy Adam, repeat his sin and die. Oh no. Paul's saying we share in Adam's sin. We were *there.* Just as later he'll say we *share in* Christ's death. There, too.

v17: thru' Adam, death reigns over us. So you'd expect Paul to say that thru' Jesus, life reigns. Yeah? But it's even better than that: we ourselves get to share in Jesus' reign.

v18-21: it helps to look out for the 'just as... so also' phrases.

• *What three comparisons is Paul making here?*

v13-14: 'cos of sin, death was let loose on everyone. v13 doesn't mean that sin didn't matter before the law was given (by God to Moses). Rather the law showed sin up so that we could recognise it for what it is, and recognise ourselves for what we are - sinners in need of Jesus. Look at v20-21.

• *What was the result of the introduction of the law?*

• *What did this in turn lead to?*

TWIN PEAKS

Paul's reply to v1: 'God's grace not only forgives sin, but delivers us from sinning.' Superb. So live showing this is true.

v3-4: pretty much all believers at this time were baptised when they started to trust Jesus. It demonstrated their faith.

Hey, push yourself. Pick out 8 stages in the development of Paul's argument: v 1-2, 3, 4-5, 6-7, 8-10, 11,12-13,and 14.

• *What if Jesus hadn't been raised from the dead?*

v14: 'under law': ie, accepting an obligation to keep it - and so being condemned for not keeping it; 'under grace': ie, acknowledging you're dependent on the cross of Christ.

Our illustration was twins. It could be books: volume 1 (our old self) is closed. Vol 2 is open. Don't re-open vol 1. OK?

Optional extra

SLAVERY - A WAY

Get the thrust of this passage? Keep reminding yourself who *you are* as a Christian: you've been united with Christ (v1-14) and become a slave of God (v15-23). So live like it, folks. Repeat after us: 'I'm a new person in Christ, and by his grace I shall live accordingly.' Got that?

v15 (as v1) is not an abstract objection that's got no relevance to us. Ever felt the temptation: 'Go on! Continue in sin. Feel free! God will forgive you.'

• *How will you use Romans ch. 6 to combat that next time?*

Christians are slaves to obedience (v16), to righteousness (v18), to God (v22).

• *Why do you think Paul uses these expressions rather than just saying 'slave to God' every time?*

Trusting Jesus (becoming a Christian) is an act of self-surrender (v16). So, of course, it leads to slavery to God. Slavery demands a radical, total obedience.

• *What challenge does Matthew 6 v24 lob at you?*

TWO WEDDINGS AND A FUNERAL

In ch. 7, Paul's big discussion point is the law. In fact, the law (also called 'the written code' or 'commandment') gets mentioned in each of the first 14 verses. And it appears 35 times between 7 v1 and 8 v4. Bet you didn't know that.

v1: it's as if he's replying to another objection to his teaching - those who say 'How can Paul just dismiss God's law the way he does? Outrageous!' Paul's reply in ch. 7 is this:

1. Paul says Christians are 'released' from the law (v1-6);

2. Paul defends the law (v7-13);

3. Paul points out the weakness of the law (v14-25).

v4: same idea as we've seen already in 6 v2-4.

v6: the Spirit's not mentioned again until 8 v2. Is that significant? We think so. Wait and see!

LAW ON TRIAL

In all, Paul's pretty neutral about the law: sure it's God's law (v12, 14), but it's unable to save anybody (v19).

There's a big debate about Romans ch. 7. The question is:

• *Who's the 'wretched man' in v24 and the 'I' of v14-25?*

• *Is it Paul? And if so, as a) an unconverted Jew; b) one in the process of conversion; or c) is it Paul as a Christian?*

We opt for (b). It isn't someone completely apart from God, but he's also not yet free from slavery to sin - as a Christian surely is. Recall 6 v15-23?

Find an older, wiser Christian - and dig into ch. 7 together...

People can love church and the Bible - but their religion can still be 'law'. When we see salvation as more about following rules than trusting Jesus' rescue, we're in danger of that, too.

• *How will you avoid this trap?*

Optional extra

SPIRIT SPECIAL

v1: Paul sums up all that's gone before. As he did in 5 v1.

v3-4: the law couldn't justify us or make us holy ('cos it couldn't change our sinful natures). But God took the initiative!

Try explaining v1-4 yourself. And you can't use the words: condemnation, sin, righteous, rumbustious, law, or ostrich.

v5: our 'mindset' (our pre-occupations, ambitions, drive) reveals our basic nature as Christians or non-Christians.

• *What does yours say about you?*

v11: Christ's resurrection is the pledge and pattern of ours.

There's a kind of life which leads to death.

There's a kind of death which leads to life. See this in v13?

Rooting out sin isn't a case of 'let go and let the Spirit do it.' No, he enables us to do it (v13). So do so.

Let v17 sink in: we're heirs of God. We'll share his glory! More on this in the next study.

GROAN ZONE

'Christians are those who have been saved, who are being saved and who will be saved.' See all this in Romans 8?

v20a: see God's curse on the world in Gen 3 v17-19.

v22: 'pains as of childbirth': ie, they're not just intense pains (ask your mum), but they show a new order *is* coming.

It's said: 'Some Christians grin too much and groan too little.'

• *Do you think that's right?*

• *What about your expectations, then?*

v23: we're *longing* for our bodies to be transformed (no more pain) and our selfish natures to be destroyed (no more sin).

v26-27: it's not talking about us issuing grunts or groans. Just saying: God's Spirit prays for us. And he too longs for the day when we'll be free from our present sufferings. Brilliant!

ALL FOR SURE

God's pledge is not that suffering won't touch us. It's that it won't separate us from his love. Take that to heart.

v29-30: 'Foreknew' = knew us intimately before creation. 'Predestined' = decided upon beforehand.

Isn't this unfair on those God doesn't choose? No. We all reject God and all deserve the worst. But because God is merciful he not only sends Jesus to die for us, but also makes it impossible for some of us to keep on rejecting him.

v30: see the 'chain' stretching from eternity to eternity.

• *What assurance must this give every Christian?*

All who are justified by faith (chs. 3-4) have great privileges: peace with God (ch. 5), union with Christ (ch. 6), freedom from law-keeping (ch. 7) and life with God's Spirit (ch. 8).

• *What's been the highlight of chs. 1-8 for you?*

Optional extra

1 KINGS

DAD'S LADS

Welcome to the eye-opening OpExworld of 1 Kings.

1 & 2 Kings are best taken as one story (just like 1 & 2 Sam).

1 Kings grabs the story from 2 Sam 20 v22 and looks lke this:

Chs. 1-2: End of David, start of Sol's rule

Chs. 3-11: Sol's rule

Chs. 12-14: The kingdom split

Chs. 15-16: Civil war between Israel and Judah

Chs. 17-22 (and on into 2 Ki 1): Ahab's rule and Elijah.

Read the verses not covered in the study (ie, v15-27, 36-40).

v6: Cold, old and not bold: David failed to correct his children. Proverbs 22 v6 is a truth worth storing in your head.

v33: a horse or mule was a status symbol.

• *So what do Zec 9 v9 and Matt 21 v1-11 tell us about Jesus?*

v37: now see Matt 12 v42b. Fantastic, huh?

v50: the altar's 'horns' were a place of refuge.

POWER SHOWER

v4's a big verse in Kings. Unfortunately, David's descendants blew it and didn't live like this. As the rest of the book shows.

v3: 'walk before God' crops up a lot in 1 Kings (hey, it's a phrase taken from Deut). What's it mean, do you think?

• *Could it be said to characterise your way of life?*

Please snaffle the bits we missed: v26-27, 34-45. Cheers.

OK, boldly we name and shame the troublemakers:

v5-6: *Joab* murdered Abner (2 Sam 3 v27) and Amasa (2 Sam 20 v8-10) in peacetime. Mmm, nice kind of bloke.

v8: *Shimei* cursed David (see 2 Sam 16 v5-16, 19 v16-23). And cursing God's chosen king earned the death penalty.

Why didn't David kill 'em off himself? Dunno. He should have.

v15, 22: Ad claimed to submit to God's authority (v15b) while asserting his own will (v16). That's impossible.

• *At what point do your actions contradict your faith?*

SOL'S SOLO

Please gulp down the bits we missed: ch. 4 v1-19, 22-28. Ta.

3 v1: this marriage was the start of Sol's spiritual downfall (wait for ch. 11). Think why it's a disaster.

3 v2: 'high places': see an OK use of one in 1 Sam 9. But see also God's instructions in Deut 7 v5, 12 v3.

• *What were God's people to do about the religions they would encounter in Canaan?*

• *What would happen if they failed to take this action?*

3 v2: 'the Name': ie the presence, character and glory of God.

3 v6-9: Sol prayed with humility, thankfulness, and trust.

• *Would these describe the way you pray?*

• *Will you ask God for help to carry out your duties (as v7b)?*

Optional extra

HOUSE WARMING

Walloping big chunks to read, we admit: 5 v8-18, chs. 6 &7. Think why we're given such detailed info about the temple.

This first temple was about double the size of the tabernacle (big tent thing) God had ordered to be built while his people were on the move (Ex 26). But it had roughly the same plan.

5 v4: chase the 'rest' theme from Deut 12 v10 to Heb 4 v1-11.
5 v13: forced labour? Mark of a bad king (try 1 Sam v10-18).

6 v2, 7 v2: Sol's palace was bigger than the temple. But what was it that made the temple far more significant?

8 v6: the 'cherubim' were carved, winged creatures each about 5m high, placed over the ark. They were regarded as the visible footstool of God's invisible throne.

• *See that in 2 Kings 19 v15, Psalm 80 v1, 99 v1? Oh yes!*

Scrunch 6 v11-13. What's overwhelming about the truth of God living among his people? And what's alarming about it?

HOUSE MASTER

You know the score. Read ch. 8 again, taking in the bits not included in the study: ie, v14-21, 25-26, 31-53, 62-66.

In v31-53, draw out the seven occasions when God's people would turn to him in future (see all the phrases 'When...')

• *What do almost all of them have in common?*

• *So what was the big ongoing need of God's people? Why?*

v39, 58, 61: Sol knew the heart of the human problem - right?

• *So what's exciting when we hit Heb 8 v7-12 (esp v10)?*

Answer this, please: where does God live?

• *If you were to answer in Sol's time, what would you say?*

• *If you were to answer nowadays, what would you say?*

1 Kings 8 v 14, 27: God lives in heaven and at the temple.
Ephesians 2 v19-22: God lives in heaven and in his people.
Tell God your response to this.

v41-43, 60: see the emphasis on 'all people' coming to know God? Is this your outlook, too? Or whom do you exclude?

SPICE WHIRLED

Please read ch. 9 v10-28 and ch. 10 v14-29, and think:

• *What are all these details teaching me about Sol's wisdom?*

• *See how God's words in ch. 3 v11-13 were coming true?*

9 v4: David's integrity before God would be the benchmark for assessing all kings after him. eg, 11 v6, 14 v8, 15 v3...

10 v1: Sheba was probably in Arabia, ie the Red Sea area. The questions might have been about God, but the exchange of goods (v10, 13) suggest trade business going on, too.
10 v9: great that she recognises the God of Israel, but there's not much sign of a personal faith in her.

Read Matthew 12 v42: why should we listen to Jesus' words?

Optional extra

FATAL ATTRACTION

Please fill in the gaps: read v14-25. Oh, bless'ya.

For some reason, this OE's a big one. Dunno why. Tuck in!

Catch God's warnings about inter-marrying with those who weren't members of God's people (Deut 7 v1-4, Ex 34 v16).

• *Is there a warning in this for you? About your friendships, relationships, peer group, those you mix with?*

See Sol's steps to disaster:

1. He allows himself to be led by his feelings (v1).

2. He ignores God's specific written commands (v2) ...

3. ... repeatedly (v3a).

4. He gives in to peer pressure (v3b).

5. He finds his loyalties are divided (v4).

6. He ends up doing things which make God angry and bring his judgment on Sol (v5-8, 9).

• *Are you slipping down a slope from 1 to 6? In what?*

• *What counter-action will you take to return to pleasing God?*

And all this by the king of God's people: how much more was a greater king needed - one who'd obey God's law perfectly.

• *Remember how far Jesus' obedience went?*

Was Solomon all he's sometimes cracked up to be? Was he really the wisest guy that's ever lived?

• *What portrait does 1 Kings actually give us?*

v7: with God's temple now built, think what Sol should have done to the 'high places'. Any doubts - see Deut 12 v1-14.

v11-13: see how God's judgment is a) definite; b) thorough; c) follows warnings; d) is delayed and reduced in God's mercy.

• *What does this remind us of God's character?*

v31-32: maths muddle? You thought there were 12 tribes? You're right. From now on the tribe of Benjamin was merged with Judah - and the two were counted as one tribe. Ça va?

v36: scorcha! Sol's failure doesn't cancel God's promise to maintain a people for himself.Thank God that he kept on being bothered about his people - and that he still is. Phew.

SIDE SPLITTING

We counted seven godless blunders of Jerob in v25-33:

1. He broke the unity of God's people (v25-27);

2. He set up idols (v28);

3. He diverted people away from God's house in Jerusalem (v28-30);

4. He restored the high places (v31);

5. He made anyone a priest, contrary to God's orders (v31b);

6. He re-arranged the calendar of festivals (v32);

7. He took the priest's role himself (v32, 33).

No wonder he forfeited the promise God made him (11 v38).

• *Do we believe the Bible, the word God's given us?*

• *Are we at risk of ignoring God and just being religious?*

Rehob tried diplomacy (v18), then force (v22-24), but failed.

• *What was God's plan with this split kingdom, do you think?*

v7: a king who'd serve? There's an idea. Mk 10 v42-45, right?

Optional extra

SPEAK AND DESTROY

Go on, mind the gaps: ie, 13 v11-33, 14 v19-20, 25-31.

13 v1: what should Exodus 32 have taught Jerob?

13 v18: the false prophet lied, we're told, but was still used by God to rebuke the man of God for being disobedient.

• *What do we see of God's hand in the events of chs. 13-14?*

• *If you had to describe God from this, what would you say?*

14 v15-16: now see 2 Kings 17 v23. It was 722 BC. These things happened as God said they would. Now think:

• *Do you believe God's words about the future (ie, Jesus' return, his judgment, heaven and hell) will come true?*

• *Why should we?*

14 v15: Asherah poles - like flag poles? No. They were symbols of a fertility goddess. Burn 'em, God said (Deut 12 v3).

14 v21b: why should Rehob have behaved much better?

GO IT, POET

15 v1-8, 16-24, 33-34, 16 v7-28 are all yours. Grab 'em!

15 v3: now check James 1 v5-8. Get the drift, do you?

16 v23-24: first Shechem, then Tirzah, but from now on, Samaria would be the capital of the northern kingdom Israel.

16 v31: Ahab disobeyed God in marrying Jezebel because she was not an Israelite. His attempt to serve two masters -

God and Baal - led to the downfall of his kingdom.

See this principle on an individual level: read Matt 6 v19-24.

• *Honestly speaking, whom are you serving?*

• *Is it possible to have divided loyalties, says Jesus?*

• *What follows when we start to consider sins 'trivial' (16 v31)?*

• *What's the only remedy for this?*

16 v34: stupid. Hiel should have known better (Joshua 6 v26).

JAW JAH JAR

Chs. 17-22 recount the reign of Ahab and his successors and their confrontation with God's outspoken prophets, like Elijah.

v1: famine as a sign of God's punishment. Recall 8 v35-36?

v1: ha, ha, catch this. Baal was (it's thought) worshipped as a storm god, a god of rain. See what God brought (v1b)?

Chs. 17-18 show Baal's ineffectiveness - and God's power.

• *In ch. 17, what does God have control over?*

Read James 5 v17-18: what are we to copy from Elijah?

Why were there miracles of God at this point?

Well, in the Old T, God acted in a direct, supernatural way often when his people were in national crisis (eg, the plagues in the conflict with Pharaoh and his gods - Ex 7-11)..

The miracles would show God's unrivalled ablility and remind his people to trust him. Reading about them, will we do so?

• *How does John 20 v29-31 encourage us?*

Optional extra

FIRE PROOF

Contrast v3 with 2 Sam 21 v1.

- *What marked David out when famine struck?*

v3: it's a different Obadiah (no, not this one) who gave his name to the Old T book. No connection. Just so you know.

v21: ie, 'get off the fence.'

- *How might you re-phrase v21's challenge for your friends?*
- *With v39, what will you now say to your friends who are religious but not Christian?*
- *Why should everyone turn to the God revealed in the Bible?*
- *How does the sacrifice of 1 Kings 18 point us to the cross?*

v22: a *single* prophet, Elijah, challenged the *whole* nation to return to God. There were other prophets (as in v4 and in chs. 19, 20 & 22) - but at this point only Elijah's gone public.

v27: Elijah taunts them that Baal's just acting like a human. ('Busy' here could mean 'gone to the loo'...)
Contrast the living Lord God in Psalm 121 v1-4.

v33-35: Elijah wants to make sure there are no accusations that he's cheating (by pouring on petrol etc).

v36-37: pick out Elijah's two calm requests.

- *What needed to happen to God's people (v37b)?*
- *Doesn't it still? Don't you need to pray this?*

v40: as God had said (Deut 13 v5, 13-18).

FEEL IT BURN

- *Why's it healthy to do business with God alone (as v3)?*
- *What's the danger if we don't?*

v4: 'It's not up to us to ask for death, but for life.' Agree? Why?

v5-8: think what God's provision might remind Elijah of.

- *How would this help him keep going as God's prophet?*

v8-13: Horeb (or Sinai) was where God met Moses and delivered the Ten Commandments. See the parallels:
40 days/nights: Ex 34 v28.
God action in nature: Ex 19 v9, 16.
God's presence: Ex 34 v6.
Covering his face from God: Ex 33 v20-22.
ie, Elijah's the new Moses, calling his people back to God's ways, as Moses did. Er, wowsville.

v19-22: we don't meet Elisha again until 2 Kings 2 v1.

- *What has ch. 19 taught you about the way God deals with his servants? How does this affect you?*

BIG BEN'S HIGH NOON

Please fill in the gaps: **read v5-12.**
We like v10: 'there'll be too many of us to pick up the rubble.'
And v11: 'yeah, right, don't count your chickens, matey...'

v13, 28: both battle accounts underline the fact it's Ahab's last chance to show whether he'd obey God's word brought to him by the prophets.

Optional extra

So ch. 20 prepares us for the death of Ahab (ch. 22) and for God abandoning a rebellious Israel that, under some appalling leadership, had abandoned him.

• *How patient is God with his people, as seen in ch.20?*

v22: ie, 'success mustn't lead us to self-confidence.'

• *What will be the inevitable result if it does?*

• *Who or what are you relying on? Honestly?*

v35-40: stories catch people off guard.

• *Remember 2 Sam 12 v1-10?*

v34, 42: what comment would you make on Ahab's action after you've read Deut 7 v1-2, 20 v16-18?

But isn't this wipe-out order from God uncalled for? Not at all.

• *What do the verses in Deut actually teach us?*

NAB THY NEIGHBOUR

v19: of course, it happened like this. See 22 v38.

v23: ditto ditto, ditto ditto ditto ditto. See 2 Kings 9 v30-37.

• *What is 1 Kings teaching us about God's words?*

v13: 'outside the city' to avoid pollution, but a place of disgrace. As in Nums 15 v36, Acts 7 v58 and Hebs 13 v11-13.

• *What does the Hebrews bit remind us about Jesus?*

We'll give you a minute to talk about Jezebel. Ready? Go!

• *What do you make of her (16 v29-34, 19 v2, 21 v5-15, 23)?*

• *What did God make of her? Why?*

WAR OF WORDS

Stonkettes! For the final time, please knock back the bits we missed in the study. It's v41-53. Cheers. You're a gem.

• *Diff between true and false prophets?*

It's v6 and v14: false prophets aimed to please Ahab rather than speak the truth.

• *Diff between a good king and a bad one?*

Ahab refused to submit to the authority of God's word (v8, 18). Jehosh, did, however (v5, 43).

One lesson from 1 Kings for us (who live after Jesus) is this:

• *What's our attitude to what God's said - his written word?*

• *When it challenges you hard, do you fight it, try to pretend it's not addressing you - or calmly recognise God's authority?*

• *What will be your attitude from now on?*

v18: somebody said 'It's a common human reaction to try to silence the word of God when it decrees judgment.'

• *When have you known this to be true?*

• *Have you faced up to the Bible's words on God's judgment?*

Watch for The Ichthus File on 2 Kings. It picks up the story of:
the prophets Elijah and Elisha (19 v19-21);
God's judgment on Ahab's family (21 v21-22);
God's judgment on Ahaziah (22 v51-53);
the exile and abandoning by God of Israel (14 v15-16);
God's protection of his true people (11 v36, 19 v18).
And more! So hang on. First, thank God for 1 Kings, right?

The Bible fair and square

The Ichthus File No 17: Romans 1-8, 1 Kings, Psalms.

St Matthias Press

P.O.Box 665, London SW20 8RU England

Tel: (0181) 947 5686 Fax: (0181) 944 7091

Radstock Ministries

2a Argyle Street Mexborough South Yorkshire S64 9BW

Tel: (01709) 582345 Fax: (01709) 583202

Registered Charity 326 879

ISBN 1-873166-47-8

Issue 17 of The Ichthus File was hand-crafted by:

Editor: Al *'Ivory towers'* Horn

Publisher: Tim *'Racket rocket'* Thornborough

Minutes man: Ian *'Stainless'* Bull

Big cheese: Steve *'Mixer'* Timmis

Pic picker: Martin *'SW'* Cole

This issue's contributors:

Julian *'Hoole Cool'* Mann, Steve *'sounds like warden'* Couch

OK, boffsters, where do we all live then?

If you correctly place all seven names, we'll give you a free... no, we won't. We'll keel over and pretend to be gobsmacked.

• *Going to take up the challenge?*

And there's more. Try these:

• *If knees were backwards, what would chairs look like?*

• *If an orange is orange, why isn't a lime called a green?*

• *How come we never use the word 'gruntled'?*

The Ichthus File. Satisfy your big-time tingles.